NEEDLECRAFT
PRESENTS

NEEDLECRAFT PRESENTS

Sixty gifts to make at home

edited by Pam Darlaston

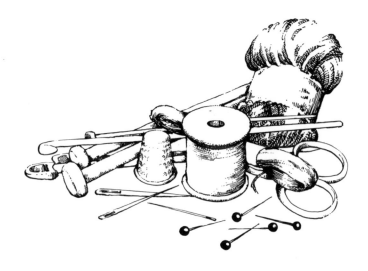

David & Charles

Newton Abbot   London   North Pomfret (Vt)

Colour photography by Tony Griffiths, Photography 2000

Line illustrations by Elaine Franks

British Library Cataloguing in Publication Data

Needlecraft presents: sixty gifts to make at home
1. Needlework
I. Darlaston, Pam
746.4   TT705

ISBN 0-7153-8688-3

Phototypeset by Typesetters (Birmingham) Ltd
Smethwick, Warley, West Midlands
and printed in Great Britain
by Redwood Burn Limited, Trowbridge
for David & Charles (Publishers) Limited
Brunel House   Newton Abbot   Devon

Published in the United States of America
by David & Charles Inc
North Pomfret   Vermont 05053   USA

Contents

Introduction   7

Knitting   9
Knitted flowers · King of the castle jumper · Aran handbag · Nursery cushions · Child's Fair Isle hat, mittens and leg warmers · Embroidered shawl · Little cat jersey · Mohair beret

Lace and Tatting   31
Circular tatted mat · Lacemaker's bobbin case and pincushion · Bobbin lace picture · Fenella the fairy · Embroidered net handkerchief · Bobbin lace number motifs

Crochet   41
Ladies' moccasins · Doily · Ring shawl · Ladies' jumper · Santa pot · Pâté-toast cover · Under-plate doily · 'Coconut Ice' child's tabard · Child's jacket

Appliqué and Quilting   57
Personalised pillowcase · Baby's quilt · Cat cushion · Motif cushion · Child's neck purse · Little Red Riding Hood play cushion

Patchwork   69
Owl cushion cover · Hexagon patchwork cushion · Petal cushion · Needlecase and pincushion · Tote bag · Commemorative cushion · Cathedral window patchwork evening bag · Cathedral window patchwork needlecase

Sewing and Embroidery   95
Embroidered robin Christmas card · Toddler's hooded top · Embroidered greetings cards · Tapestry panel · Reversible play cloak · Nursery picture – Goosey Goosey Gander · Strawberry workbox · Decorative handbag · Party bag · Applied embroidered fabric picture · Full-fringed tablecloth and napkins

Bazaar Bestsellers   125
Cheshire and Isle of Wight cottage pincushions · Smocked lavender sachet · Play-and-learn collage · Padded hanger with potpourri heart · Appliquéd fabric box · Suffolk puff clown · Strawberry emery · Peg bag · Heart-shaped brooches · Christmas decorations · Play apron · Knitting bag and needle roll · Hand-printed scarf

Introduction

Never be lost for ideas for presents again. Here are lots of suggestions – something for everyone. There's the opportunity, too, to try a new needlecraft; if you are an expert knitter, try your hand at lacemaking or tatting; if dressmaking is your favourite craft, why not work some crochet for a change.

There are surely solutions here for your Christmas present problems. Some of the gifts can easily be made by a child for granny and there are dozens of small items which will make ideal fund raisers for bazaars and fêtes. For something really different which could be handed down through the family, make the commemorative cushion on page 86. How satisfying to enjoy knitting a jumper, working a lace picture or weaving a tapestry panel and then have the pleasure of giving it to someone special.

Abbreviations

GENERAL

st	stitch
rep	repeat
beg	beginning
inc	increasing
dec	decreasing

KNITTING

k	knit
p	purl
st	stitch
tog	together
yf	yarn forward
tbl	through back of loop
foll	following
alt	alternate
st st	stocking stitch
g st	garter stitch
M1	make one stitch by picking up horizontal thread lying in front of next stitch on left-hand needle and knit into back of it

sl	slip
psso	pass slipped stitch over

LACE

prs	pairs
WS	whole stitch
HS	half stitch

TATTING

st	stitch
lp	loop
cl	circle
ch	chain
jl	join loop
j	join

CROCHET

ch	chain
ss	slipstitch
dc	double crochet
tr	treble
dtr	double treble
tr tr	triple treble
sp	space
yrh	yarn round hook

Transferring patterns

A design can be transferred to fabric in a number of ways:

1 Using a washable transfer pencil or tailor's pencil, draw directly on to the fabric round templates, etc.

2 Tack paper or card shapes into position. Tack round them, outlining the shapes, then remove the papers.

3 Pin and tack paper pattern to fabric, cut round edges.

4 Place dressmaker's carbon (available in different colours) between the fabric and design and draw over the outlines with a sharp pencil. Make sure that the fabric, carbon and design are firmly anchored.

5 A special transfer pencil can be used to trace the design, which is then ironed on to

the fabric. Often, the design will be reversed.

Enlarging patterns
1 Trace the outline from the book on to tracing paper.
2 Rule a grid of squares all over. Number the squares.
3 Take a sheet of paper the final size required and rule a grid of squares all over, the same number of squares as the first grid. Number the squares.
4 Draw in the design, copying whatever is in each square of the small grid to the corresponding larger square. Use a dark felt pen or ink so that the enlarged outline can be easily traced and transferred to fabric.

Stuffings and glues
Various stuffings are available – kapok, foam chips, polystyrene granules, old tights. The stuffing chosen must depend on the present and its use, whether it is to be washable, whether a smooth finish is required, etc. Care must be taken to use the correct glue for the materials you are working with. Read the instructions on the tube carefully – for example, some glues can dissolve polystyrene.

Safety
Particular care should be taken when making presents for babies and young children. Washable fabrics are desirable, felt eyes are safest but if 'real' eyes are preferred, use special safety eyes. Avoid sharp edges and make sure that everything is sewn on securely. Paints used for children's gifts must be non-toxic.

Knitting

colour photographs on pages 25 and 26/7

Knitted flowers   10

King of the castle jumper   11

Aran handbag   14

Nursery cushions   14

Child's Fair Isle hat, mittens and leg warmers   18

Embroidered shawl   20

Little cat jersey   22

Mohair beret   30

Knitted Flowers

Mrs Gilbert, Shaftesbury, Dorset

Brighten up dull winter days by knitting these delightful flowers. They can all be made from the oddments of leftover yarn in your knitting basket.

Materials

Small balls of double knitting (DK) wool in red, yellow, white and green
Small ball of 4 ply wool in blue
Oddment of fine wool in black
Pair 3¾mm (No 9) knitting needles
Fine crochet hook
French knitting reel
Lengths of wire

Method

POPPY

Using red DK cast on 48 sts.
1st to 6th rows: *K4, p4, rep from * to end.
7th row: *Sl 1, k1, psso, k2 tog, p2 tog, p2 tog tb1, rep from * to end.
8th to 10th rows: *K2, p2, rep from * to end.
11th row: *K2 tog, p2 tog, rep from * to end.
12th row: *P2 tog, rep from * to end.
Break off yarn and thread through rem 6 sts, draw up and fasten off. Join the seam.
Using crochet hook and fine black yarn, * make 17 ch, work 1 dc into 2nd ch from hook, 1 dc into next 14 ch, ss into last dc, rep from * 4 times more, fasten off.
Sew centre securely into middle of poppy.

DAISY

Using white DK cast on 36 sts.
Work 4 rows st st.
Next row: K1, * yf, k2 tog, rep from * to last st, k1.
Work 5 rows st st.
Next row: Form petals by knitting together 1 st from needle and 1 loop from cast on edge, all along row.
Next row: K1, * k2 tog, rep from * to end.
Next row: P.
Next row: K1, * k2 tog, rep from * to end.
Next row: * P2 tog, rep from * to end.
Break off yarn and thread through rem 5 sts, draw up and fasten off. Join the seam.

Using yellow DK cast on 3 sts.
Working in st st, inc 1 st at each end of next and following alternate row.
Work 5 rows st st.
Dec 1 st at each end of next and following alternate row.
Next row: P.
Cast off.
Sew the centre into middle of petals.

MARIGOLD

Using yellow DK cast on 49 sts.
1st row: K.
2nd row: (Right side) * k1, yf, k2, sl 1, k2 tog, psso, k2, yf, rep from * to last st, k1.
3rd row: P.
Rep last 2 rows twice more.
Next row: * K2 tog, rep from * to last st, k1.
Next row: * P2 tog, rep from * to last st, p1.
Next row: * K2 tog, rep from * to last st, k1.
Break off yarn and thread through rem 7 sts, draw up and fasten off. Join the seam.
Using crochet hook and fine black yarn make 4ch, ss to form ring.
Next round: * 16ch, 1dc into ring, rep from * 6 times more.
Sew centre securely to marigold.

BLUEBELLS (make 7 bells per flower)

Using blue 4 ply cast on 20 sts.
1st to 5th rows: * K2, p2, rep from * to end.
6th row: * K2 tog, p2 tog, rep from * to end.
Break off yarn and thread through rem 10 sts, draw up and fasten off securely. Join the seam.

STEMS

Using French knitting reel and green DK work the required number of 30cm (12in) lengths of French knitting.
Cut wire into 35cm (14in) lengths and bend over 2.5cm (1in) at each end to form hooks. Thread wires through French knitting tubes and fasten the hooks at each end. Sew a stem to each flower.

King of the Castle Jumper

Jane Wyatt, Wendover, Buckinghamshire

Just right to appeal to any little boy's imagination, this super jersey with its castle motif is for the more experienced knitter.

Materials
100g double knitting in blue
75g of same in grey
50g of same in black
20g of same in green
Small balls of white and brown
Pair 3¼mm (No 10) needles
Pair 4mm (No 8) needles

Measurements
To fit chest 61cm (24in)

Tension
22 sts and 26 rows to 10cm (4in) measured over pattern

Method
FRONT
Using 3¼mm needles and green cast on 72 sts.
Work 2.5cm (1in) k1, p1 rib.
Change to 4mm needles *.
Reading odd numbered rows from right to left and even numbered rows from left to right and beg with a k row, work in st st and pattern from chart A, shaping as indicated.

BACK
Work as given for front to *.
Now continue as for front but working from chart B.

SLEEVES
Using 3¼mm needles and green cast on 36 sts.

Work 5cm (2in) k1, p1 rib, inc 1 st at end of last row: 37 sts.
Change to 4mm needles and blue.
Beg with a k row, work in st st inc 1 st each end of 3rd and every following 6th row until there are 49 sts.
Work straight until sleeve measures 24cm (9½in) or length required, ending with a p row.

Shape top
Cast off 4 sts at beg of next 2 rows.
Dec 1 st each end of every row until 29 sts remain.
Work 2 rows straight.
Dec 1 st each end of next and every following 4th row until 23 sts remain, then every following alternate row until 21 sts remain.
Work 1 row.
Cast off 3 sts at beg of next 4 rows.
Cast off remaining 9 sts.

NECKBAND
Join right shoulder seam.
With right side facing, blue yarn and 3¼mm needles pick up and k 15 sts down left side of neck, 20 sts across centre front neck, 15 sts up right side of neck and 30 sts across back neck: 80 sts.
Work 5cm (2in) in k1, p1 rib.
Cast off loosely in rib.

To make up
Join left shoulder and neckband seam.
Sew in sleeves, then join side and sleeve seams.
Fold neckband in half to wrong side and ss into place.

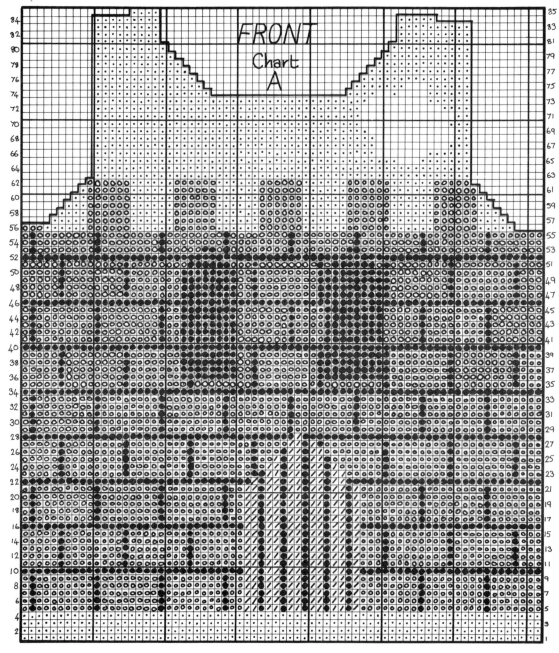

FRONT
Chart
A

BACK
Chart
B

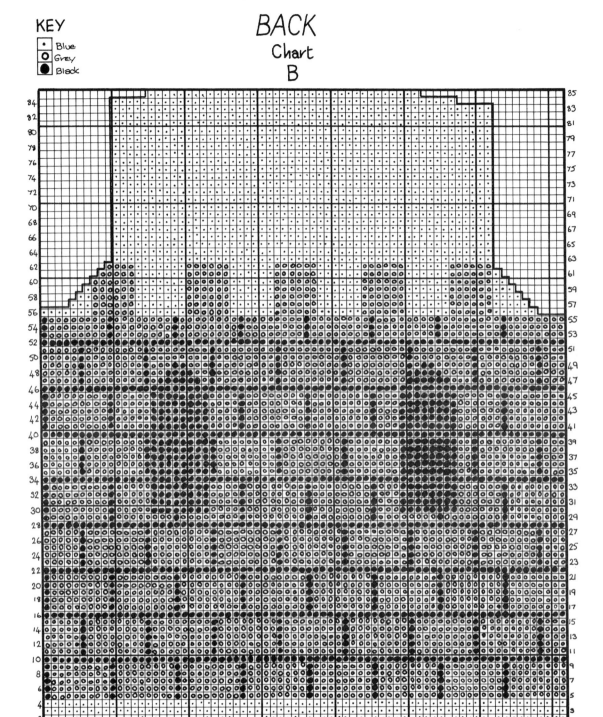

Aran Handbag

Margaret Shaw, Clitheroe, Lancashire

Use any of your favourite stitch patterns to knit the basic rectangular length of fabric used to make this novel handbag. A second length of knitting can be used for the handle. Both pieces of knitting are stiffened using heavy-duty, iron-on interlining and the handbag is completed with a sewn-in lining and a feather and polished pebble for decoration.

Materials

Two sections of knitting, one 20×36cm (8×14in) for bag and one 3×45cm (1¼×18in) for handle
Two pieces of heavy-duty iron-on interlining or plastic 'canvas' the same size
Two pieces of lining same size as above

Method

Iron on the interlining (if used) to the cover and tack to the lining of both the main piece and handle. Alternatively tack lining and main fabric to plastic canvas.
Assemble the bag by folding along the lines indicated and insert the strip to form side gussets and handle.
Oversew into position.
Sew on decoration.

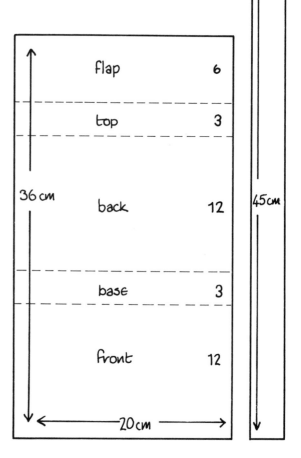

Nursery Cushions

Pauline Fryatt, Shildon, County Durham

A quick and inexpensive way to brighten up a nursery. Use bold eye-catching colours for the letters and motifs against bright or light coloured backgrounds. A choice of three motifs has been given here or you may like to substitute a favourite one of your own.

Materials

50g double knitting for front
50g same for back
Oddments for motifs

Pair 3¼mm (No 10) needles
Cushion pad or filling

Method

Using 3¼mm needles cast on 65 sts for front.
Beg with a k row, work 10 rows in st st.
Using a separate ball of yarn for each area of colour and twisting yarns at back of work when changing colour to avoid a hole, work 72 rows of pattern from chosen chart.

Work a further 10 rows in st st.
Cast off.
Using 3¼mm needles cast on 65 sts for back of cushion.
Work 92 rows st st. Cast off.
Join 3 sides of cushion. Insert cushion pad or filling.
Sew 4th side of cushion.
Make 2 pompoms by cutting out 2 circles of

card approximately 5cm (2in) in diameter.
Cut out a smaller hole in centre (Fig 1).
Using small lengths of yarn, wind yarn round cardboard circles, as shown, until hole is almost filled (Fig 2).
Cut round outer edge of yarn and tie a length of yarn securely round centre (Fig 3).
Remove cardboard rings and fluff out pompom.

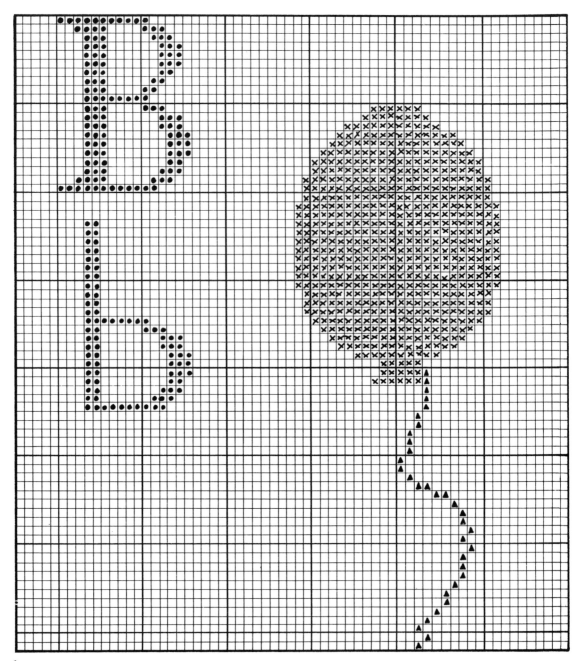

To make a bobble

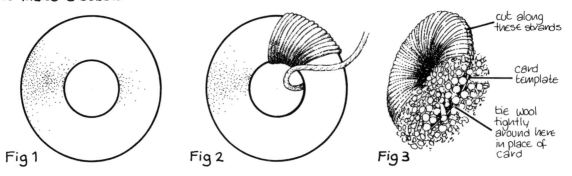

Fig 1

Fig 2

Fig 3

cut along
these strands

card
template

tie wool
tightly
around here
in place of
card

17

Child's Fair Isle Hat, Mittens and Leg Warmers

Sarah Orr, Broxburn, West Lothian

Soft background colours enhance the bold flower motifs on this child's accessories set. The simple shapes are quick and easy to knit, and make a lovely present for a little girl.

Materials

Hat – 25(35)g brushed double knitting in main colour

Small balls of same in 5 contrast colours

Mittens – 20g brushed double knitting in main colour

Small balls of same in 5 contrast colours

Leg warmers – 25(35)g brushed double knitting in main colour

Small balls of same in 5 contrast colours

Pair 3¼mm (No 10) needles for smaller size

Pair 4mm (No 8) needles for larger size

Measurements

To fit up to 3 years (3–4 years)

Tension

26 sts and 30 rows to 10cm (4in) over st st

Note

For larger size of mittens and leg warmers make as for smaller size, but use 4mm needles for working st st sections. Carry yarns not in use loosely across back of work.

Method

HAT (small size)

Using 4mm needles and main colour cast on 99 sts and work 4 rows g st.

Beg with a k row, work in pattern from chart 1 for 34 rows.

Next row: Continuing in pattern from chart, ★ k7, k2 tog, rep from ★ to end.

Work straight to row 40 on chart.

Continuing in main colour only shape top as follows:

1st row: ★ K6, k2 tog, rep from ★ to end.

2nd and every alternate row: P.

3rd row: ★K5, k2 tog, rep from ★ to end.

5th row: ★ K4, k2 tog, rep from ★ to end.

7th row: ★ K3, k2 tog, rep from ★ to end.

9th row: ★ K2, k2 tog, rep from ★ to end.

11th row: ★ K1, k2 tog, rep from ★ to end.

13th row: ★ K2 tog, rep from ★ to end: 11 sts.

15th row: ★ K2 tog, rep from ★ to last st, k1.

Cut off yarn leaving a long end, thread through rem sts, draw up tightly and secure.

HAT (larger size)

Using 4mm needles and main colour cast on 108 sts and work 4 rows g st.

Beg with a k row work in pattern from chart 1 for 36 rows.

Next row: Continuing in pattern from chart, ★ k7, k2 tog, rep from ★ to end: 96 sts.

Work straight to row 44 of chart.

Continuing in main colour only, work 4 rows st st.

Shape top

1st row: ★ K6, k2 tog, rep from ★ to end: 84 sts.

Work 3 rows straight.

5th row: ★ K5, k2 tog, rep from ★ to end.

Work 3 rows straight.

9th row: ★ K4, k2 tog, rep from ★ to end.

10th and every following alternate row: P.

11th row: ★ K3, k2 tog, rep from ★ to end.

13th row: ★ K2, k2 tog, rep from ★ to end.

15th row: ★ K1, k2 tog, rep from ★ to end.

17th row: ★ K2 tog, rep from ★ to end.

19th row: ★ K2 tog, rep from ★ to end: 6 sts.

Cut off yarn leaving a long end, thread through rem sts, draw up tightly and secure.

To make up

Join back seam.

Make a tassel out of short lengths of all colours used and stitch to top of hat.

MITTENS (both alike)

Using 3¼mm needles and main colour, cast on 34 sts.

Work 12 rows k1, p1 rib.

For larger mittens, change to 4mm needles.

Beg with a k row work in pattern from chart 2 for 2 rows.

Keeping pattern correct, shape for thumb as follows:

Next row: K16, M1 (by picking up horizontal thread lying between st just worked and next st on left-hand needle), k2, M1, k16.

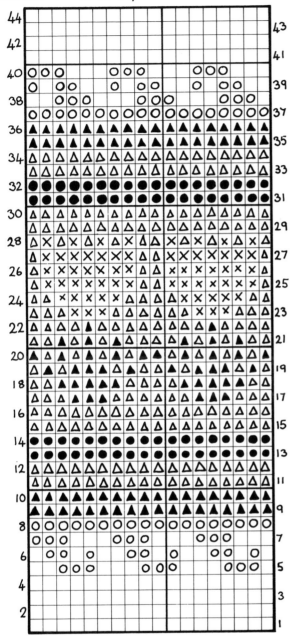

CHART 1   18 st repeat

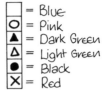

KEY

☐ = Blue
○ = Pink
▲ = Dark Green
△ = Light Green
● = Black
✕ = Red

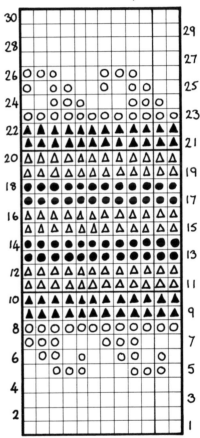

CHART 2   12 st repeat

Work 5 rows in pattern from chart.
Next row: Pattern 16, M1, pattern 4, M1, pattern 16.
Next row: P.
Next row: Pattern 16, M1, pattern 6, M1, pattern 16.
Next row: P 40 sts.
Either working thumb in one colour only or in stripes as given on chart, continue as follows:
Next row: Pattern 24, turn and cast on 1 st.
Next row: P9, turn and cast on 1 st.
Work 11 rows on these 10 sts.
Next row: (P2 tog) 5 times.
Cut yarn leaving a long end, thread through remaining thumb sts, draw up and secure.

Join seam to base of thumb.

With right side of work facing, join yarn to last st on right-hand needle, pick up and k 2 sts from base of thumb, then k to end: 34 sts. Continuing in pattern from chart, work in st st for a further 11 rows.

Shape top

Next row: ★ K2, k2 tog, tb1, k10, k2 tog, rep from ★ once, k2.
Next row: P.
Next row: ★ K2, k2 tog, tb1, k8, k2 tog, rep from ★ once, k2.
Next row: P.
Next row: ★ K2, k2 tog, tb1, k6, k2 tog, rep

from ★ once, k2.
Cast off. Join side seam.

LEG WARMERS (both alike)
Using 3¼mm needles and main colour, cast on 50 sts.
Work 8 rows k1, p1 rib.
For larger leg warmers, change to 4mm needles.
Beg with a k row, work 44 rows from chart 1.
For larger leg warmers, change back to 3¼mm needles.
Work 8 rows k1, p1 rib.
Cast off in rib.
Join back seam.

Embroidered Shawl
Pamela Pavitt, Upper Norwood, London

An elegant shawl which you can make to any size or thickness you wish. Add embroidery and fringing to match or contrast with the basic shawl making it suitable for everyday wear or a special occasion.

Materials
Several balls of required yarn plus a pair of suitable needles for that yarn
Note: To estimate how large to make the shawl if using oddments of yarn, keep increasing until half the yarn has been used, then work the decreasing with the other half of yarn.

Method
KNIT THE TRIANGLE
Cast on 6 sts and working in st st, inc 1 st at the same edge on every row until required depth is reached (or half the yarn has been used).
Work 2 rows, then dec 1 st on shaped edge on every row until 6 sts remain.
Cast off.

MAKE HEM
Using reverse st st side as right side, turn back a hem onto right side down straight edge and tack into place.
Using either matching or contrasting yarn, stitch hem into place with zig-zag chain stitch as shown in Figs 2 and 3.

FRINGE
Cut lengths of yarn to same length by winding round a book or piece of card. Attach to both shaped edges of shawl using a crochet hook as shown in Fig 5, using 2, 3 or 4 lengths of yarn at a time to achieve required thickness of tassel.

EMBROIDERY
Using single or double strands of yarn embroider flowers using lazy daisy stitch as shown in Fig 6. Fig 4 shows finished design.

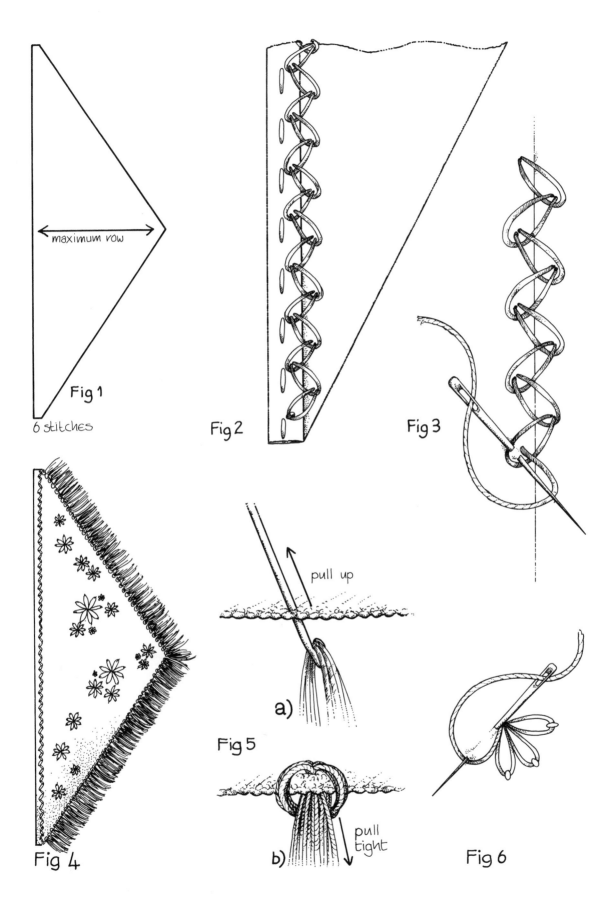

maximum row

Fig 1

6 stitches

Fig 2

Fig 3

Fig 4

pull up

a)

Fig 5

b)

pull tight

Fig 6

Little Cat Jersey

Geraldine Middleton, Dereham, Norfolk

Unusual trimmings turn this little jersey into something special. The delightful cat motif is sure to please any child and the jersey is completed with a back neck opening to make it easier to take on and off.

Materials

100g ball double knitting yarn in main colour
Small ball same in contrast colour
3 small buttons
Pair 3mm (No 11) needles
Pair 3¾mm (No 9) needles
Black embroidery thread for features
Small ball, short length of ribbon and 2 small buttons for trimmings

Measurements

To fit chest 53cm (21in)

Tension

24 sts and 32 rows to 10cm (4in) measured over st st

Method

BACK
Using 3mm needles cast on 54 sts.
Rib row: ★ K1, p1, rep from ★ to last 2 sts, k2.
Rep this row 9 times more.
Change to 3¾mm needles.
Next row: K.
Next row: K1, p to last st, k1.
Rep these 2 rows until 60 rows st st have been worked.

Shape raglans
Cast off 3 sts at beg of next 2 rows.
Next row: K2, sl 1, k1, psso, k to last 4 sts, k2 tog, k2.
Next row: K1, p to last st, k1.
Rep these 2 rows until 36 sts remain, ending with a p row.
Divide for back neck opening.
Next row: K2, sl 1, k1, psso, k16, turn leaving rem 16 sts on a spare needle.
Next row: K4, p to last st, k1.
Next row: K2, sl 1, k1, psso, k to end.
Next row: K4, p to last st, k1.

Rep these 2 rows once more.
Next row: (Buttonhole row) k2, sl 1, k1, psso, k to last 4 sts, k2 tog, yf, k2.
Next row: K4, p to last st, k1.
Continuing dec at raglan edge as before, work a further 10 rows, working another buttonhole on the 7th row.
Leave rem 11 sts on a safety-pin.
Return to sts on spare needle.
Rejoin yarn, cast on 4 sts, k to end.
Complete to match first side of neck, omitting buttonholes and reversing shaping.

FRONT
Work as given for back until 6 rows of st st have been worked.
Using small balls of yarn for each area of colour and twisting yarns together when changing colour to avoid a hole, proceed as follows:
Next row: K28 main colour, 4 contrast, k to end in main colour.
Continue in this way working from chart until cat motif is complete, then continue as given for back until 30 sts remain during raglan shaping.

Shape neck
Next row: K2, sl 1, k1, psso, k8, turn leaving rem sts on spare needle.
Next row: P2 tog, p to last st, k1.
Next row: K2, sl 1, k1, psso, k to last 2 sts, k2 tog.
Rep last 2 rows once more.
Keeping neck edge straight, continue dec at raglan edge as before until 2 sts remain, ending with a p row.
K2 tog and fasten off.
Return to sts on spare needle.
Slip first 6 sts on to a safety-pin, rejoin yarn to remaining sts, then complete to match first side of neck reversing all shaping.

SLEEVES
Using 3mm needles cast on 34 sts.
Work 10 rows k1, p1 rib as given for back.
Change to 3¾mm needles.
Working in st st as given for back, inc 1 st each end of 3rd and every following 8th row

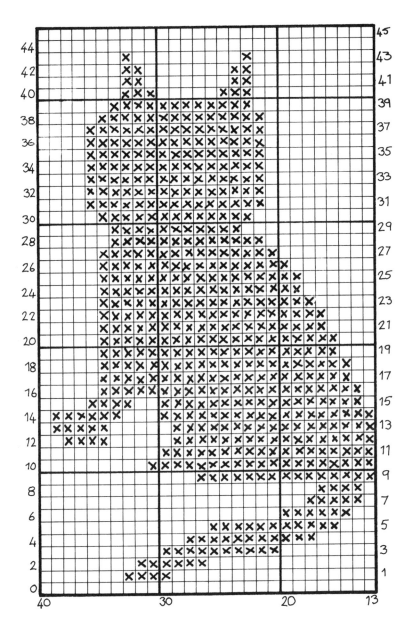

until there are 42 sts.
Continue in st st until 60 rows have been worked.

Shape raglan
Cast off 3 sts at beg of next 2 rows.
Work 2 dec rows as given for back until 6 sts remain, ending with a p row.
Leave these sts on a safety-pin.

NECKBAND
Join raglan seams.
With right side of work facing and 3¾mm needles, pick up and k 11 sts from left back neck, 6 sts from left sleeve, 12 sts down left front neck, 6 sts across centre front, 12 sts up right front neck, 6 sts from right sleeve and 11 sts from right back neck: 64 sts.
Next row: K4, ★ k1, p1, rep from ★ to last 4 sts, k4.
Rep this row 4 times more, working a buttonhole as before on 3rd row.
Cast off in rib loosely.

To make up
Join side and sleeve seams.
Catch down lower edge of button band, sew on buttons.
Embroider whiskers and sew on eyes, ribbon and bell as illustrated.

23

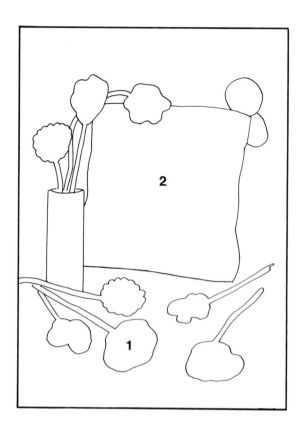

KNITTING *(opposite)*
1 Knitted flowers *(page 10)*
2 Nursery cushion *(page 14)*

KNITTING *(overleaf)*
1 King of the castle jumper *(page 11)*
2 Little cat jersey *(page 22)*
3 Child's Fair Isle hat, mittens and leg warmers *(page 18)*
4 Embroidered shawl *(page 20)*
5 Mohair beret *(page 30)*
6 Aran handbag *(page 14)*

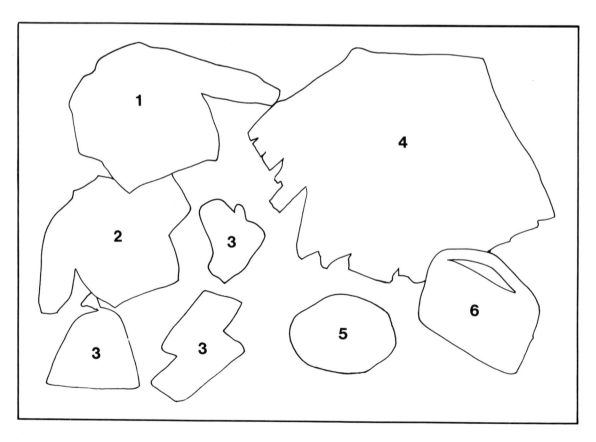

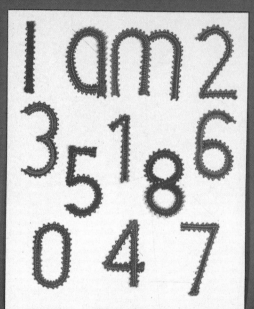

LACE AND TATTING *(opposite)*
1 Embroidered net handkerchief *(page 38)*
2 Circular tatted mat *(page 32)*
3 Bobbin lace number motifs *(page 40)*
4 Lacemaker's bobbin case and pincushion *(page 33)*

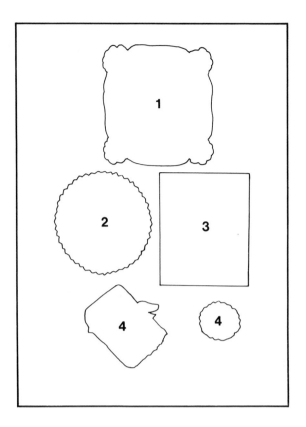

Mohair Beret

Penny Burnfield, Stockbridge, Hampshire

A very attractive hat, knitted in a multicoloured mohair yarn with one of the colours picked out by the swirling stripes which radiate from the centre. It is very quick and easy to knit and as it uses very little yarn inexpensive to make.

Materials

Two 25g balls of medium-weight mohair yarn in main colour (M)
1 ball same in contrast colour (C)
Set of four 4½mm double-pointed needles
Set of four 3¾mm double-pointed needles

Tension

20 sts and 26 rows to 10cm (4in) measured over st st

Method

Note: Before commencing knitting, wind off 5 small balls of C approximately 3m (3¼yd) long and 1 ball 3.5m (3⅞yd) long.
Using the 3.5m (3⅞yd) ball of C and 4½mm needles cast on 12 sts and divide them between 3 needles (4 sts on each).
Round 1: Using the spare needle, k to end.
Round 2: (Using M, M1, using C, k2) 6 times.
Round 3: (Using M, M1, k1, using C, k2) 6 times.
Round 4: (Using M, M1, k2, using C, k2) 6 times.
Joining in the separate small balls of yarn, one for each stripe, continue as follows:
Round 5: (Using M, M1, k3, using C, k2) 6 times.
Continue inc in this way, knitting 1 more st between contrast stripes on every row until:
Round 14: (Using M, M1, k12, using C, k2) 6 times. (30 sts on each needle.)
Now inc on alternate rows as follows:
Round 15: Keeping stripes correct, k to end.
Round 16: (Using M, M1, k13, using C, k2) 6 times.
Continue inc 1 more st between contrast stripes on every alternate row until:
Round 28: (Using M, M1, k19, using C, k2) 6 times. (44 sts on each needle.)
Round 29: Keeping stripes correct, k to end.
Rounds 30 to 37: As round 29.
Now shape brim as follows:
Round 38: (Using M, k18, k2 tog, using C, k2) 6 times.
Round 39: Keeping stripes correct, k to end.
Round 40: (Using M, k17, k2 tog, using C, k2) 6 times.
Round 41: As round 39.
Continue dec in this way working 1 less st between each contrast stripe on every alternate row until:
Round 46: (Using M, k14, k2 tog, using C, k2) 6 times. (34 sts on each needle.)
Cut off main colour and all short lengths of contrast yarn.
Join in main ball of C.
Change to 3¾mm needles.
Work 4 rounds k1, p1 rib.
Cast off in rib.

To make up

Using length of contrast yarn, gather up central hole and fasten off securely.
Carefully darn in all ends.

Lace and Tatting

colour photographs on pages 28 and 45

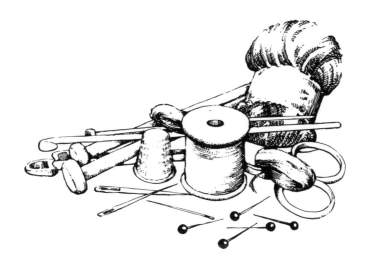

Circular tatted mat   32

Lacemaker's bobbin case and pincushion   33

Bobbin lace picture   34

Fenella the fairy   36

Embroidered net handkerchief   38

Bobbin lace number motifs   40

Circular Tatted Mat

Jackie Hirst, Abingdon, Oxfordshire

Worked in basic stitches this is a fairly simple mat for a beginner to attempt. The same stitch sequences are repeated over and over again to form a very pretty design.

Materials
1 ball fine cotton
Tatting shuttle

Method
CENTRE RING
Make 12 cls of 4 sts, jl, 4 sts, lp, 4 sts, lp, 4 sts, connected by 12 chs of 4 sts, lp, 4 sts.

SIX SURROUNDING RINGS
Each of 8 cls of 4 sts, jl, 4 sts, lp, 4 sts, lp, 4 sts, connected by 8 chs of 6 sts, lp, 6 sts one of which must be joined to a ch of centre ring.

NEXT ROUND
(Starting between two rings)
cl 4 sts, lp, 4 sts, lp, 4 sts, lp, 4 sts
ch 4 sts, lp, 4 sts, lp, 4 sts, lp, 4 sts
cl 6 sts, jl, 6 sts
ch 4 sts, lp, 4 sts, lp, 4 sts, lp, 4 sts
cl 4 sts, jl, 4 sts
ch 4 sts, lp, 4 sts, lp, 4 sts, lp, 4 sts
cl 6 sts, jl, 6 sts
ch 4 sts, lp, 4 sts, lp, 4 sts, lp, 4 sts
Repeat this pattern 6 times more.

FINAL ROUND
cl 4 sts, jl, 4 sts, lp, 4 sts, lp, 4 sts
ch 4 sts, lp, 4 sts
cl 4 sts, jl, 4 sts, jl, 4 sts, lp, 4 sts
ch 4 sts, lp, 4 sts
Repeat this pattern 23 times more.

To make up
Dampen and pin out until dry.
If necessary press with a hot iron.

Abbreviations

st	stitch		
l	loop		
cl	circle	eg	worked from shuttle
ch	chain	eg	worked from bobbin
j	join	eg	

Lacemaker's Bobbin Case and Pincushion

Mrs S. A. Eddy, Penzance, Cornwall

The perfect gift for a lacemaker, somewhere to keep both pins and bobbins safe and decoratively as well. This bobbin case and pincushion can be made completely out of the oddments in your work basket.

BOBBIN CASE

Materials

30cm (12in) piece of floral cotton at least 65cm (25½in) wide
Same size piece of plain cotton
Same size piece of polyester wadding
1¼m (1½yd) of gathered lace edging, 1½cm (⅝in) wide
75cm (29½in) ribbon, 25mm (1in) wide

Method

Begin by drawing up pattern as illustrated.

1   Using pattern, cut once in floral cotton, once in plain cotton and once in wadding.

2   Take floral piece and starting at point A (1½cm [⅝in] in from edge), pin and tack lace edging round outside, upper edge to point B (10½cm [4¼in] from bottom edge), easing round corners and positioning edging with straight edges and right sides together and lacy edge towards centre of material.

3   With right sides together pin and tack contrast plain fabric to floral, sandwiching lace in between.

4   Place wadding on top of material pieces, pin and tack.

5   Machine round case, through all thicknesses, wadding uppermost, leaving a gap in the lower edge for turning.

6   Trim seams and corners and turn work through to right side.

7   Slip stitch gap to close and press lightly.

8   Tack through all thicknesses 9cm (3½in) from bottom edge and machine along this line.

9   With contrast piece uppermost make a turn up on machine line and ss edges of pocket thus formed to outer edge and flap end, where they touch.

10   Divide pocket into 12 sections, each section approximately 4.3cm (1⅝in) wide, pin, tack and machine through all thicknesses, starting at the bottom edge to the top of each section.

11   On right side of case find centre of flap edge. Find point in ribbon 25cm (10in) in from end and sew at this point to centre flap edge.

12   Roll bobbin case and wrap longer length of ribbon round and tie in a bow.

13   For a personal touch, embroider initials at bottom corner of flap.

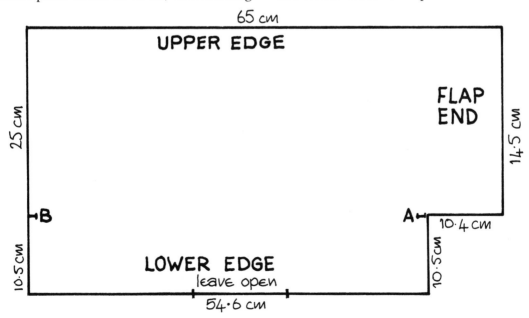

PINCUSHION

Materials
Scraps of cotton material
Narrow ribbon and lace edging
Polyester filling
Thin card
UHU glue

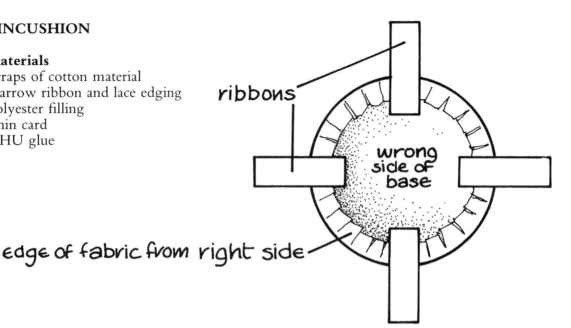

ribbons

wrong side of base

edge of fabric from right side

Method
1 Cut three 5cm (2in) circles of card and glue together to form base. Leave to dry.
2 Cut one 7cm (2¾in) circle of fabric and stick centrally to base circles. Snip edges, turn and glue to wrong side of base.
3 Cut four 5cm (2in) lengths of narrow ribbon. Fold in half and glue to wrong side of base at equal intervals leaving 1½cm (⅝in) protruding from edge of base. (These ribbons are used to pin the cushion to the lace pillow so ensure that they are secure.)

4 With right side upwards, glue lace edging round wrong side of base, letting edge of lace protrude over the base and hide the ribbon pieces. Leave to dry and ensure that all pieces are secure before continuing.
5 Cut a 12cm (4¾in) circle of fabric and gather near edge. Pull up gathers enclosing a ball of filling. Fasten off gathering threads, adding more filling if necessary.
6 Glue underside of cushion to wrong side of base. Leave to dry.

Bobbin Lace Picture
Averil Hylton, Sprowston, Norwich, Norfolk

This lovely picture of a little girl is worked using mainly Honiton lace techniques but as it uses only simple stitches it can be worked by anyone with a basic knowledge of bobbin lace. The instructions for the filling stitches have not been given as these can be found in any basic bobbin lace book.

Materials
Pillow
28 pairs bobbins
Threads in an assortment of colours

Method
BONNET
1 Start by hanging 4 prs on a pin at A, work in WS twisting workers three times round pin on each side. Add prs as ribbon widens, and as ribbon narrows to become bonnet band discard bobbins to leave 5 prs. Work bonnet band to within 3 pinholes from end. Leave 1 bobbin out on each side, continue to end. Tie all prs 3 times then lay them back over completed work. Bind with the 2 bobbins discarded earlier.

2 Work second ribbon in WS, starting at point with 4 prs. Add and discard prs as necessary. Finish by sewing prs into side of 1st ribbon, tie 3 times and cut off.

3 Sew 4 prs into band at B and work outer edge of bonnet in rib. At bonnet ribbons

DRESS

Start at F with 3 prs and work in HS as for arm. Add prs as necessary and sew workers into pinholes along side of apron. Discard prs as you near the top, finish by sewing into apron.

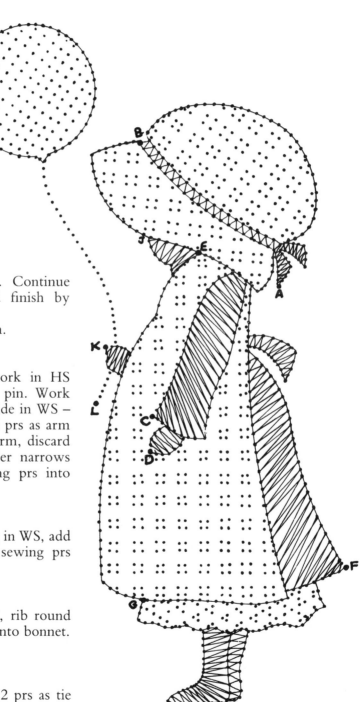

sew in workers as you cross. Continue round bonnet back to B and finish by sewing prs into side of band.

4 Work filling stitch – blossom.

ARM

Start at C with 4 prs and work in HS twisting worker 3 times round pin. Work passive pr nearest pin on each side in WS – this keeps the edge firm. Add 6 prs as arm widens. Continue working up arm, discard approximately 4 prs as shoulder narrows and finish by sewing remaining prs into bonnet.

HAND

Hang 3 prs on pin at D, working in WS, add prs as necessary, finishing by sewing prs into arm.

APRON

1 Sew 4 prs into bonnet at E, rib round apron and finish by sewing prs into bonnet.
2 Work filling – jubilee.

APRON TIE

Start at point with 4 prs. Add 2 prs as tie widens, finish by sewing into apron.

PETTICOAT

1 Sew 4 prs into pinhole G. Rib round lower edge of petticoat finishing by sewing prs into dress.
2 Work filling – honeycomb.

FEET

Work complete foot first in WS starting at toe with 4 prs and increase prs to about 10 prs at widest part. Work up leg if necessary discard 1 or 2 prs. Finish by sewing remaining prs into petticoat.

2ND LEG

1 Sew 2 prs into pinhole H and hang 3 prs on pin I. WS up 2nd leg sewing the worker into pinholes of 1st leg on one side. Add 1 pr of bobbins as leg widens if necessary.
2 Finish by sewing prs into petticoat.

FACE

Sew 3 prs into pinhole J. Work in WS adding prs as necessary. Finish by sewing prs into apron.

SECOND HAND

Start at K by hanging 3 prs on pin. Work in WS adding and discarding prs as necessary. Finish by sewing prs into apron.

BALLOON

Hang 4 prs on pin at L, rib to hand. Sew prs into nearest 2 pinholes. Twist prs together across hand, sew prs into 2 pinholes on opposite side of hand. Continue to rib up balloon string and round outside of balloon. Sew prs into balloon string at base of balloon to complete circle. Use these prs to commence. Pin and stitch filling.

To complete

After removing all pins turn to right side, place onto suitable colour backing material and put into picture frame.

Fenella the Fairy

Susan Fisher, Lynmouth, Devon

A delightful picture, worked in very fine filet crochet which is attractively displayed by being mounted against a dark background.

Materials

1 reel Coats Sewing Cotton in white
0.60mm steel crochet hook
A piece of navy blue felt 20×25cm (8×10in)
Picture frame 20×25cm (8×10in)

Tension

13 blocks or spaces and 14 rows to 5cm (2in)

Method

Commence by making 121ch.
1st row: 3ch (to count as first dtr), 1dtr into each ch to end: 122dtr.
2nd row: 3ch, 1dtr into each of next 6dtr, *[2ch, miss 2dtr, 1dtr into next dtr] 8 times, 1dtr into each of next 3dtr *, rep from * to *, 1dtr into each of next 3dtr, rep from * to * twice more, 1dtr into each of last 3dtr.
Continue in pattern from chart, working 4dtr for each single block with 3dtr for each extra block and 2ch, 1dtr for each space, until all 58 rows are worked.
Fasten off.

To make up

Soak piece of crochet in a solution of cold water starch.
Remove and squeeze out excess.
Pin and block out work to measure 15×20cm (6×8in)
Allow to dry thoroughly before removing pins.
Place crochet in centre of felt, place frame over crochet and secure into position.

KEY ☒ 4 dtr ☐ 1 dtr, 2 ch, 1 dtr

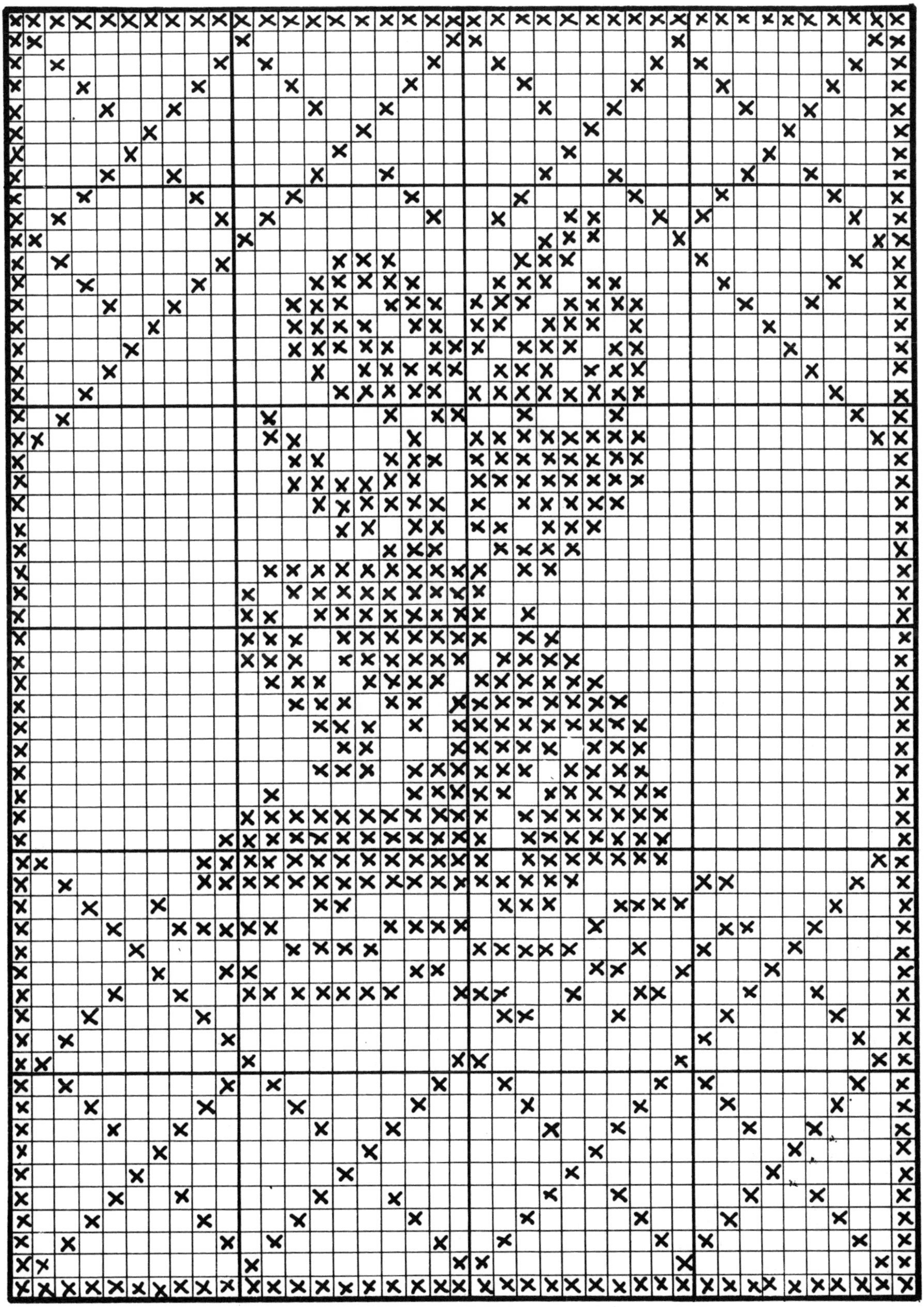

Embroidered Net Handkerchief

Edna Groves, Newport, Isle of Wight

A beautifully worked lace handkerchief edge, without the time-consuming method of bobbin or needlepoint lace. This lace is woven onto a background of purchased net fabric, giving the impression of far more elaborate work.

Materials

30cm (12in) square of coloured cotton for backing

20cm (8in) square of white cotton for handkerchief

Stranded embroidery cotton

Method

Trace the pattern onto the coloured cotton backing.

Tack the net on top with small sts, and outline the pattern, just outside the drawn line.

Make sure when working the embroidery that you 'pick up' only the net and do not catch the pattern underneath.

First of all work around the outlines using double cotton and running stitch (Fig 1), picking up alternate threads of the net.

To fill the leaves, whip over the diagonal lines of holes (Fig 3), picking up each 'hole' of the net in rotation using alternate rows and working down 1 row and up the next. When all embroidery is completed, take care to darn all ends in carefully.

TO WORK THE FLOWER

Work 2 rows of running stitch (Fig 2) to each line of the net for the petal edge.

Fill the petals with cobweb stitch (Fig 5), worked on the horizontal line of the net.

Work over 3 horizontal rows picking up alternate holes from the top to the bottom row, working from right to left.

Turn the work round so that the needle is on the right again and work another row; the bottom line of holes from the first row is the first row of holes of the next 3. Finish the filling in this way.

The centre is worked in whipping stitch, similar to the leaves, but take three stitches into alternate holes as you work down the net (Fig 4), turn the work and repeat.

To make up

Remove from the coloured cotton backing.

Work one row of close blanket stitch round the edge of the pattern.

Tack the net to the 20cm (8in) square of cotton, work 3 rows of chain stitch as close as possible to the first one, level with the square line of double cotton.

Remove the tacking.

With sharp scissors, trim the net away round the outside edge. Trim the cotton away along the back of the work as close as possible to the back of the chain stitch, then trim the net away at the front.

quarter pattern

1 Running Stitch, use double cotton for the outlines

2 Running Stitch, use single cotton for the petal edge
Two rows of running to each row of holes

3 Whipping, rows of diagonal stitches worked on the diagonal line of the net

4 Whipping, three stitches into alternate holes, working on the diagonal of the net

5 Cobweb Stitch, worked on the horizontal lines of the net, from right to left

Bobbin Lace Number Motifs

Moira Gray, East Kilbride, Glasgow

Use these motifs to sew on dresses, sweaters and so on for a child's birthday surprise. The lace is intricately worked to form a firm tape which can be attached easily to most fabrics.

Materials

Fil à Dentelle thread
9 prs of bobbins

Method

1 Working from the number of your choice, start where indicated in diagram, working in cloth stitch to right and left. When a corner is reached take your weaver through to the middle, do not put pin in.

2 Use the last pair of bobbins, pass through and weave back to outside. Repeat to the centre not working through the last pair. Do not pin. Work back to outside edge. You should now have 2 prs not working in centre. Repeat until point is reached, then turn pillow round and proceed to work back in pairs to point where corner began. Continue until number is complete.

3 After working last pin, tie weaver pr once, holding the pr in your left hand, place right hand bobbin under left on pillow.

4 Pick up next bobbin on right, knot, put right-hand bobbin under left bobbin on pillow.

5 Continue to end, knot twice, put left-hand bobbin under right-hand bobbin, place on pillow, pick up next bobbin on left, knot, putting left-hand bobbin under right-hand bobbin. Continue until end. Cut ends off closely.

40

Crochet

colour photograph on pages 46/47

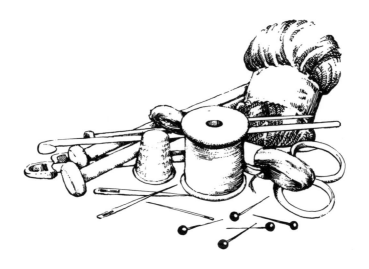

Ladies' moccasins   42

Doily   50

Ring shawl   50

Ladies' jumper   51

Santa pot   52

Pâté-toast cover   53

Under-plate doily   54

'Coconut Ice' child's tabard   54

Child's jacket   55

Ladies' Moccasins

Mrs J. Beverley, Pontefract, West Yorkshire

Soft and comfortable to wear at home, easy to pack when going away, these slippers are a lovely gift for a friend. This pair are decorated with beads but you could add a motif or decoration of your own choice or even leave plain.

Materials
200g dishcloth cotton
3.00mm crochet hook

Measurements
To fit shoe sizes 4/5 and 6/7

Method
SOLES
Commence with 10ch.
Row 1: 1dc into 2nd ch from hook, 1dc into each ch to end.
Row 2: 2ch (to count as first dc), 1dc into each dc to end: 10dc.
Rows 3 to 6: As 2nd.
Row 7: Inc in first st, 1dc into each dc to last st, inc in last st: 12dc.
Rows 8 to 11: Work straight in dc.
Row 12: As row 7: 14 sts.
Rows 13 to 16: Work straight in dc.
Row 17: As row 7: 16 sts.
Rows 18 to 21: Work straight in dc.
Row 22: As row 7: 18 sts.
Rows 23 to 31: Work straight in dc.
Row 32: As row 7: 20 sts.
Rows 33 to 46: Work straight in dc.
(For larger size work 4 extra rows dc)
Row 47: Work 2dc tog, 1dc into each st to end: 19 sts.
Row 48: Work in dc to end.
Row 49: As row 47: 18 sts.
Row 50: Work in dc to end.
Row 51: As row 47: 17 sts.
Row 52: Work in dc to end.
Row 53: Work 2dc tog, 1dc into each st to last dc, turn.
Row 54: Work 2dc tog, 1dc into each st to last 2dc, turn: 12dc.
Row 55: Ss across 3dc, 1dc into each st to last dc, turn: 8dc.
Row 56: Work 2dc tog, 1dc into each of next 4dc, ss into each of next 3dc, fasten off.
Work 3 more sole pieces in same way.

UPPERS
Make 103(111)ch loosely, ss to first ch to form ring.
Round 1: 3ch, 1tr into each of next 13tr, 1htr into each next 10ch, 1dc into next 55(63)ch, 1htr into next 10ch, 1tr into next 14ch, ss to top of 3ch.
Round 2: 3ch, 1tr into next 21sts, 1htr into next 6sts, 1dc into next 47(55)sts, 1htr into next 6sts, 1tr into last 22 sts, ss to top of 3ch.
Rounds 3 to 5: As round 2. Break off cotton.
Next row: With right side facing, rejoin cotton to first of 22tr worked on previous row, 3ch, 1tr into each of next 43tr, turn.
Next row: 3ch, 1tr into each tr to end.
Next row: As last row. Fasten off.
Turn down the last 2 rows to make a casing, fasten down by working ss through both thicknesses.
Fasten off.
Make a 2nd piece in the same way.

TOE CAP
Make 12ch.
Row 1: 2dc into 2nd ch from hook, 1dc into each of next 9ch, 2dc into last ch: 14 sts.
Row 2: Inc in first st, 1dc into each dc to last st, inc in last st: 16 sts.
Row 3: As row 2: 18 sts.
Rows 4 to 7: Work in dc to end.
Row 8: 3ch, 1tr into each st to end.
Rows 9 to 20: Work in dc to end.
(For larger size work 4 rows extra)
Row 21: Working in dc, dec 1st each end of row: 16 sts.
Row 22: Work in dc to end.
Row 23: As row 21: 14 sts.
Row 24: Work in dc to end.
Row 25: As row 21: 12 sts.
Row 26: Work in dc to end.
Row 27: As row 21: 10 sts.
Rows 28 to 30: As row 21: 4 sts.
Fasten off.
Make a 2nd piece in the same way.

To make up
Place 2 sole sections together (see diagram).
Place a marker on each side of sole between rows 24 and 25 counting from the heel.

Pin upper to sole, placing markers directly below the end of the cuff (see diagram).
Pin rest of upper evenly round sole.
Join yarn to corner of heel, working through upper and both soles, work 1 round of dc right round slipper to opposite corner of sole.
Working through all 3 thicknesses, work 10dc across heel, turn.
Work 11 rows dc to form heel gusset. Fasten off.
Stitch gusset into place at back of slipper.

Pin toe cap into place (see diagram), join yarn to right hand side of slipper and work 1 row of dc, working through both thicknesses. Fasten off.
Using 3 lengths of cotton each 2m (2¼yd) long make a twisted cord.
Starting halfway along treble row on toe cap, thread cord through front of slipper, through casing and back through treble row to front of slipper. Tie into a bow.
Sew on beads or embroider motif of your own choice.

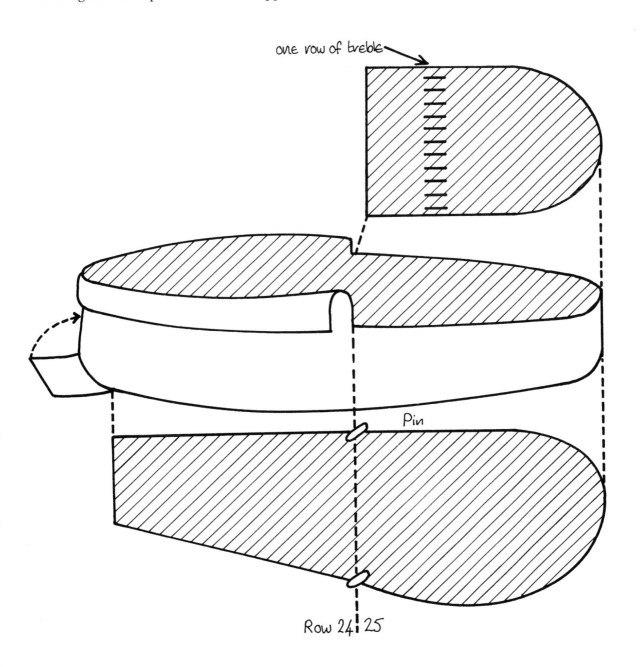

one row of treble

Pin

Row 24 25

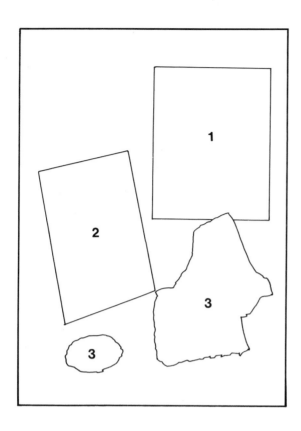

LACE AND TATTING (opposite)
1 Fenella the fairy (page 36)
2 Bobbin lace picture (page 34)
3 Lacemaker's bobbin case and pincushion (page 33)

CROCHET (overleaf)
1 Ring shawl (page 50)
2 Child's jacket (page 55)
3 Ladies' jumper (page 51)
4 Ladies' moccasins (page 42)
5 Under-plate doily (page 54)
6 Pâté-toast cover (page 53)
7 Doily (page 50)
8 'Coconut Ice' child's tabard (page 54)
9 Santa pot (page 52)

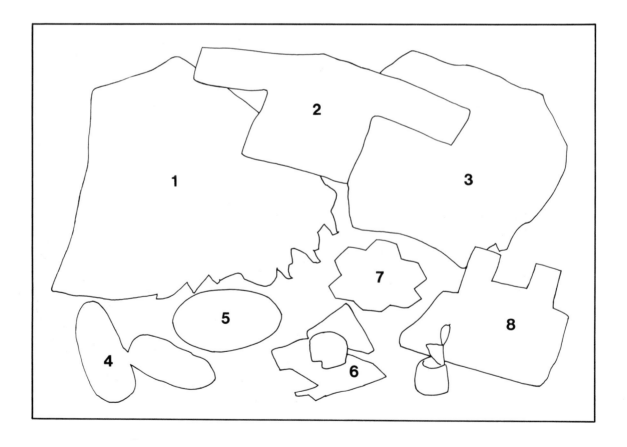

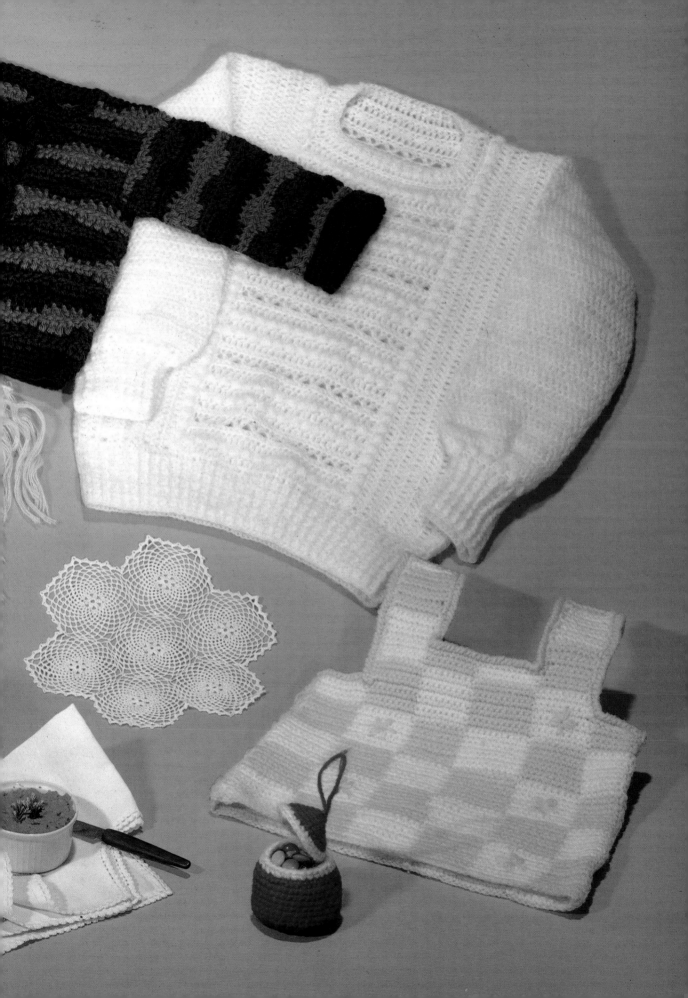

APPLIQUÉ AND QUILTING *(opposite)*
1 Motif cushion *(page 62)*
2 Little Red Riding Hood play cushion *(page 64)*
3 Personalised pillowcase *(page 58)*

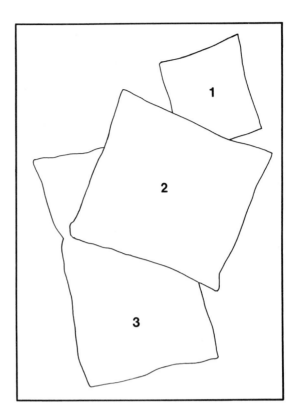

Doily

Sheila Evans, Pontyberem, Llanelli, Dyfed

Pretty enough to grace any coffee table, this little doily is made up from seven motifs which are joined together in their final round. A dainty picot edging is worked round the outer edge to complement the swirling design.

Materials
One 20g ball of Coats Mercer Cotton No 20
1.25mm crochet hook

Measurements
Finished doily is 25cm (10in) in diameter

Method
FIRST MOTIF
Make 8ch, ss to first ch to form ring.
1st round: 3ch, keeping last loop of each st on hook, work 2dtr into ring, yrh, draw through all loops on hook – called a 2dtr cluster, ★ 3ch, 3dtr cluster into ring, rep from ★ 4 times more, 3ch, ss to top of first 3ch.
2nd round: ★ 3ch, 1dc into next st, rep from ★ to end.
3rd round: Ss to centre of first loop, ★ 3ch, 1dc into next loop, rep from ★ to end.
4th to 6th rounds: As 3rd.
7th round: As 3rd working 4ch instead of 3ch.
8th to 10th rounds: As 7th round working 5ch instead of 4ch.
11th round: Ss to centre of first loop, ★ 9ch, 1dc into next loop, [5ch, 1dc into next loop] 3 times, rep from ★ to end.
Fasten off.
Make 6 more motifs, join to other motifs on the 11th round as follows:
11th round: Ss to centre of first loop, 4ch, ss to 9ch loop of first motif, 4ch, 1dc into next loop, work as for first motif to next 9ch loop, join as before.

BORDER
1st round: Join yarn to one 5ch loop, ★ 5ch, 1dc into next loop, rep from ★ to end.
2nd round: Into each 5ch loop work [3dc, 3ch, 3dc]. Fasten off.

To make up
Damp and pin out to measurements to dry.

Ring Shawl

Gina Talbot, Dereham, Norfolk

A beautifully light and lacy shawl which, as its name suggests, is so fine that it will pass through a wedding ring. This one has been crocheted in a version of Solomon's knot pattern, a traditional stitch that is both quick and easy to work.

Materials
1 cone of very fine 1 ply wool
3.50mm crochet hook

Method
Commence with 323ch.
Foundation row: 1tr tr into 4th ch from hook, 1tr tr into each ch to end: 321 sts
1st row: ★ Lengthen the loop on hook to 8mm (⅜in), yrh and draw a loop through, insert hook into the single thread at back of loop by passing hook in front of original loop and work 1dc into it, rep from ★ once – 1 double knot made, miss 3tr tr, 1dc into next st ★★, rep from ★ to ★★ to end of row.
2nd row: Lengthen the loop on hook, insert hook into dc at centre of last double knot st worked, and work 1dc. ★ Work first half of double knot then work 1dc into centre dc of next double knot from first row – one single knot made, rep from ★ to end of row.
These 2 rows form the pattern, working dc to complete each double knot into the next 'dc knot' along the row.

Rep these 2 rows 13 more times, ending with a 2nd row, noticing that 1 double knot is decreased on every 1st row.

Next row: Work as for 1st row, but dec 1 extra knot at each end by working only a single knot at beg and end of row.

Next row: As 2nd row.

Continue dec in this way until the shawl reaches the length required.
Fasten off.

To make up
Add a fringe by cutting lengths of wool approximately 36cm (14in) long and by using 3 lengths at a time, make a tassel at every row end.

Ladies' Jumper
Pauline Fitzpatrick, Mackworth, Derby

This very delicate ladies' jumper crocheted in a soft brushed yarn would make a lovely present for anyone. It is fairly simple to work with the minimum of shaping.

Materials
8 balls Jarol Morning Cloud Brushed DK
4.00mm crochet hook
5.00mm crochet hook

Measurements
To fit bust 86–91cm (34–36in)
Length 56cm (22in)
Sleeve seam 46cm (18in)

Tension
14 tr to 10cm (4in) using 5.00mm hook

Method
BACK PANEL
Using 5.00mm hook make 31ch.
Foundation row: Work 1tr into 4th ch from hook, 1tr into each ch to end: 29tr.

2nd row: 1dc into first tr, * into next st work [yrh, insert hook into st and draw loop through] 4 times, yrh and draw through all loops on hook – called MB, 1dc into next st, rep from * to end.

3rd row: 2ch, miss first st, 1tr into each st to end.

4th row: 1dc into each st to end.

5th row: 2ch, miss first 2 sts, * into next st work [1tr, 1ch, 1tr] – called 1 V st, miss next 2 sts, rep from * 7 times, 1 V st into next st, miss 1 st, 1tr into last st.

6th row: 1dc into each st (including ch).

7th row: As 3rd row.
8th row: As 2nd row.
9th row: As 3rd row.
Rep 2nd to 9th rows 5 times more.
Fasten off.

FRONT PANEL
Work as given for back to ★.
Rep 2nd to 9th rows 4 times more.
Fasten off.
Make 2 separate lengths of 9ch and keep to one side for when joining panels.

SIDE PANELS
Join panels as follows:
With right side of front facing and using 5.00mm hook, work 1dc into each dc or bobble row end and 2dc into each tr or V st row end up side of work, work 1dc into each ch of one of the 9ch lengths then work row dc along side edge of back panel as given for front: 145dc.

Next row: As 2nd row of back panel.
Next row: As 3rd row of back panel.
Rep the last row 8 more times. Fasten off.

SLEEVES
With wrong side facing, miss the first 37 sts, rejoin yarn to next tr, 2ch, 1tr into each of next 70tr, turn.
Work 26 more rows in tr.
Next row: (dec row) ** Insert hook into next st, yrh and draw loop through, insert hook into next st, yrh and draw loop through, yrh and draw through all 3 loops on hook **, rep from ** to ** 16 times

more, [insert hook into next st and draw loop through] 3 times, yrh and draw through all 4 loops on hook, now rep from ★★ to ★★ 17 times: 35 sts.
Next row: As 2nd row of back panel.
Change to 4.00mm hook.
Work in rib as follows:
Next row: 2ch, ★ yrh, inserting hook from back round stem of next tr, draw loop through and complete tr in usual way, yrh, inserting hook from front round stem of next tr, draw loop through and complete tr in usual way, rep from ★ to end.
Next row: Work as given for last row, inserting hook from front round front raised trs and from back on trs raised at back.
Work a further 9 rows in rib. Fasten off.
Complete second side panel and sleeve to match the first.

WELTS
With right side facing and 4.00mm hook, join yarn to lower edge of front, 2ch, work 68tr evenly along lower edge.
Work 10 rows in rib as given for cuff, fasten off.
Work back welt in same way.

NECKBAND
With right side facing and 4.00mm hook, work 1 row dc round neck edge, dec 1 st at each corner.
Work 2 rows in rib, fasten off.

To make up
Join side and sleeve seams.

Santa Pot
Joni Bamford, Empingham, Rutland, Leicestershire

The ideal container for those little gifts at Christmas that are too small to wrap, or make one for every guest at a dinner party and fill with sweets. They take very small amounts of yarn and so are inexpensive to make.

Materials
Small amounts of wool in red, brown and white – preferably in chunky or thick double knitting, or you could use 4 ply double 2.50 or 3.00mm crochet hook
Note: Whatever wool you use, select a crochet hook several sizes smaller than you would usually use for that thickness of wool. It is the combination of a small hook and thick wool that gives the pot its shape and firmness.

Method
POT
Using the brown make 4ch, ss to first ch to form a ring.
1st round: Work 8dc into ring, place a marker at last st to denote end of round.
2nd round: Inc by working 2dc into each dc to end of round: 16dc.
3rd round: ★ 1dc into first dc, 2dc into next dc, rep from ★ to end: 24dc.
4th round: ★ 1dc into each of next 2dc, 2dc into next dc, rep from ★ to end of round: 32dc.
5th round: ★ 1dc into each of next 3dc, 2dc into next dc, rep from ★ to end of round: 40dc.
6th round: 1dc into each dc to end of round.
7th round: As 6th.
Break off brown and join in red.
Work a further 7 rounds on these 40dc, moulding the pot as you go so that the side of work facing becomes the outside of pot.
15th round: ★ 1dc into each of next 2dc, miss 1dc, rep from ★ to end of round: 27dc.
Break off red and join in white.
1dc into each dc to end of round, ss to first dc of round.
Fasten off.

HAT
Using red make 4ch, ss to first ch to form a ring.

1st round: Work 8dc into ring, place a marker at last st to denote end of round.
2nd round: ★ 1dc into next dc, 2dc into next dc, rep from ★ to end of round: 12dc.
3rd round: ★ 1dc into each of next 2dc, 2dc into next dc, rep from ★ to end of round: 16dc.
4th round: ★ 1dc into each of next 3dc, 2dc into next dc, rep from ★ to end of round: 20dc.
5th round: ★ 1dc into each of next 4dc, 2dc into next dc, rep from ★ to end of round: 24dc.
6th round: ★ 1dc into each of next 5dc, 2dc into next dc, rep from ★ to last dc omitting last inc: 27dc.
Break off red and join in white.
7th round: Work 1dc into each dc to end of round, ss to first dc of round. Fasten off.

To make up
Stitch hat firmly to pot for about 2.5cm (1in). Make a loop of red yarn and secure to centre of hat.

Pâté-toast Cover
Mrs J. Stokes, Evesham, Worcestershire

A very pretty cloth for a very practical purpose. With the cloth wrong side uppermost, place a plate of toast in centre of cloth, then fold the daintily edged corners of cloth over plate to cover toast.

Materials
Piece of linen 50cm (20in) square
1 ball No 20 crochet cotton
1.50mm crochet hook

Method
1 Fold square of linen into 4.
2 Cut away shaded areas as shown in diagram.
3 Neaten edges by turning a narrow hem and stitching into place.
4 Crochet edging directly into fabric as follows:
1st round: Join yarn with dc to edge of fabric, ★ 3ch, work 1dc into fabric 5mm (¼in) from last dc, rep from ★ all round edge, working [1dc, 3ch, 1dc] into each corner, ss to first dc.
2nd round: [1ch, 3tr, 1dc] into first 3ch sp, ★ [1dc, 3tr, 1dc] into next 3ch sp, rep from ★ to end, ss into first 1ch at beg of round. Fasten off.

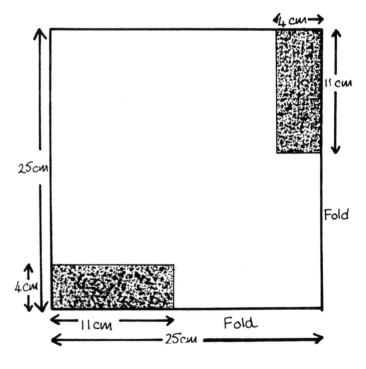

53

Under-plate Doily

Mrs J. Griffin, Kingsthorpe, Northampton

An unusual way of making a plain Pyrex plate into an attractive serving dish.

Materials

1 ball Phildar Perle No 5 cotton
1.75mm crochet hook
25cm (10in) Pyrex plate

Method

Make 8ch and join to first ch with ss to form ring.

1st round: Into ring work [1dc, 20ch] 16 times, ss to first dc (16 long loops).

2nd round: Ss to 10th ch of first loop, 1dc into loop, ★ 4ch, 1dc into next loop, rep from ★ 14 times, 4ch, ss to first dc.

3rd round: Ss into first 4ch loop, [3ch,2tr, 3ch,3tr] into same loop, ★ [3tr,3ch,3tr] into next loop, rep from ★ 14 times more, ss to top of 3ch.

4th round: Ss to centre first 3ch sp, 1dc into 3ch sp, ★ 6ch, 1dc into next 3ch sp, rep from ★ 14 times, 6ch, ss to first dc.

5th round: Ss into centre first ch sp, work as given for 4th round, working 7ch between dc.

6th round: Work as given for 5th round, working 9ch between dc.

7th round: Ss across first 3ch of 9ch loop, 1dc into loop, ★ [20ch,1dc] 4 times into same loop, 20ch, 1dc into next loop, rep from ★ 15 times omitting last dc at end, ss into first dc.

8th round: Ss to 10th ch of first loop, 1dc into loop, ★ 7ch, 1dc into next loop, rep from ★ all round, ending last rep with a ss into first dc.

9th round: Ss into centre first ch sp, work as given for 8th round, working 9ch between dc.

10th round: Ss across first 3ch of 9ch loop, 3ch to stand as first tr, ★ 2ch, 1tr into next loop, rep from ★ all round, ending with 2ch, ss into top of 3ch.

11th round: Ss into first loop, 3ch to stand a first tr, ★ 1ch, 1tr into next loop, rep from ★ all round, ending with ss into top of 3ch.

12th round: 1dc into each tr and ch of previous round.

13th round: ★ 1dc into each of first 4dc, miss 1dc, rep from ★ to end, ss to top of first dc. Fasten off.

To make up

Darn in ends, then carefully ease on over back of plate.

'Coconut Ice' Child's Tabard

Mrs M. Risborough, Priors Park, Tewkesbury, Gloucestershire

Make this attractive little girl's top in the colours of coconut ice and embroider some of the squares with toning or contrasting colours. The neck and armhole edges are finished with crab stitch and the side opening fastens to the waist with buttons.

Materials

100g double knitting in pink
100g double knitting in white
3.50mm crochet hook
4 buttons

Measurements

To fit chest 61cm (24in)

Tension

18 sts and 17 rows to 10cm (4in) over dc pattern

Method

BACK AND FRONT (alike)
Using pink and 3.50mm hook make 60ch.
Foundation row: 1dc into 2nd ch from

hook, 1dc into each of next 8ch, ★ in white, 1dc into each of next 10ch, in pink, 1dc into each of next 10ch, rep from ★ once more, in white, 1dc into each of last 10ch.

Next row: 2ch, 1dc into each dc to end, working in pink over the pink sts and white over the white sts.

Rep this last row 6 times more.

Next row: 2ch, 1dc into each dc to end, working in white over the pink sts and pink over the white sts, therefore reversing the colours.

Work in colours as set for a further 7 rows. These 16 rows form the pattern.

Continue in pattern until work measures 23cm (9in).

Shape armhole
Ss over the first 10 sts, pattern over next 40dc, turn.

Work a further 4cm (1½in) on these 40 sts.

Shape neck
Pattern across 10dc, turn.

Work straight over these 10 sts for 10cm (4in) more. Fasten off.

With right side of work facing, miss the first 20 sts at neck, rejoin yarn and pattern to end: 10dc.

Complete to match first side of neck.

To make up
Join shoulder seams. Join one side seam.

Work 1 row dc round neck edge, then 1 row crab st (dc worked from left to right), fasten off.

Work 1 row dc and 1 row crab st round armholes.

Work 2 rows dc down back side opening. Mark position for 4 buttons.

Work 2 rows dc down front side opening, working 4 buttonholes to correspond with markers as follows:

Buttonhole: Work in dc to position for buttonhole, 2ch, miss 2dc, 1dc into next st. Sew on buttons.

Embroider flowers in lazy daisy stitch at random on front.

Child's Jacket
Letitia Graham, Denny, Stirlingshire

A chunky little jacket just right for a toddler. Crocheted in a thick yarn in an unusual stripe pattern it would make the ideal gift for any child.

Materials
4 balls of Phildar Kadischa (or similar chunky yarn) in main colour A
3 balls of same in contrast colours B and C
7mm crochet hook

Measurements
To fit approximately age 3 years

Tension
10tr and 5 rows to 10cm (4in)

Method
BACK AND FRONTS (worked in 1 piece to armholes)
Using 7mm hook and A make 60ch.

Foundation row: (Wrong side) 1dc into 2nd ch from hook, 1dc into each ch to end.

Now commence pattern as follows:

1st row: In A, 3ch, miss first st, 1tr into each of next 3 sts, ★ 1dc into each of next 4 sts, 1tr into each of next 4 sts, rep from ★ to end.

2nd row: In B, 1ch, miss first st, 1dc into each of next 3 sts, ★ 1tr into each of next 4 sts, 1dc into each of next 4 sts, rep from ★ to end.

3rd row: In B, as 2nd row.
4th row: In C, as 1st row.
5th row: In C, as 1st row.
6th row: In A, as 2nd row.
7th row: In A, as 2nd row.
8th row: In B, as 1st row.
9th row: In B, as 1st row.
10th row: In C, as 2nd row.
11th row: In C, as 2nd row.
12th row: In A, as 1st row.

These 12 rows form the pattern, continue in pattern for a further 6 rows.

Divide for armholes
19th row: Keeping colour sequence correct, 1ch, miss first st, 1dc into each of next 3 sts, 1tr into each of next 4 sts, 1dc into each of next 4 sts, turn.
Continuing in pattern work 6 rows on these sts.

Shape neck
Next row: 1ch, miss first st, 1dc into each of next 3 sts, 1tr into each of next 4 sts, 1dc into each of next 2 sts, turn.
Next row: 1ch, miss first st, 1dc into next st, 1tr into each of next 4 sts, 1dc into each of next 4 sts.
Next row: 3ch, miss first st, 1tr into each of next 3 sts, 1dc into each of next 4 sts, turn.
Next row: 1ch, miss first st, 1dc into each of next 3 sts, 1tr into each of next 4 sts.
Next row: As last row.
Fasten off.

BACK
Return to main section, with right side facing and appropriate colour, miss first 4 sts, rejoin yarn and continue as follows:
Next row: 1ch, 1dc into each of next 3 sts, ★ 1tr into each of next 4 sts, 1dc into each of next 4 sts, rep from ★ twice, turn.
Continue to work over these sts, without any shaping for a further 11 rows. Fasten off.
Return to main section, miss the next 4 sts, rejoin yarn and complete to match right front, reversing shaping.

SLEEVES
Using 7mm hook and A make 28ch.
Work as given for back and fronts until 22 rows of pattern have been worked. Fasten off.

To make up
Join shoulder seams. Join sleeve seams. Sew in sleeves.

EDGING
With right side facing and A, join yarn to lower right front.
Work 1 row dc up right front, round neck, back down left front and along lower edge, working 3dc into corners, join to first dc with a ss. Work a 2nd row of dc, working 3dc into corners as before, and working 3dc evenly round neck.
Fasten off.
With wrong side of sleeve edge facing, work 2 rounds of dc.
Fasten off.

TIES (make 4)
With A make 35ch, sew in pairs to front edges.

Appliqué and Quilting

colour photographs on pages 48 and 81

Personalised pillowcase   58

Baby's quilt   58

Cat cushion   59

Motif cushion   62

Child's neck purse   64

Little Red Riding Hood play cushion   64

Personalised Pillowcase

Linda Crooks, Whaley Bridge, Stockport, Greater Manchester

An appliquéd pillowcase in crisp polyester-cotton – ideal for a child's bedroom, or make two to match your bed linen or curtains. Instead of letters, you could design your own motif.

Materials

50×80cm polyester-cotton
50×90cm polyester-cotton
scraps for coordinating fabric for letters

Method

1   Hem one short edge on each rectangle of fabric.

2   Make paper patterns for letters required and cut them out of fabric scraps. (The size of letters will depend on how many are needed.)

3   Appliqué letters to smallest rectangle, about 5cm from hemmed edge, using zig-zag stitch and matching thread.

4   Place two rectangles right sides together, folding longer piece over the appliqué to form flap. Stitch along sides and bottom edge (not appliquéd end), sewing down sides of flap at same time. Zig-zag all seams, turn through flap, and turn pillowcase right sides out.

Baby's Quilt

Linda Crooks, Whaley Bridge, Stockport, Greater Manchester

A charming gift for a new baby, with alternate pink and blue quilted squares and 'BABY' appliquéd to the front, or you could use the baby's own name. The quilt is completely machine stitched and measures approximately 56×82cm.

Materials

twelve 16cm squares pink polyester-cotton
twelve 16cm squares blue polyester-cotton
coordinating fabric for letters (each 12cm
   high)
58×84cm   white   polyester-cotton   for
   backing
58×84cm wadding

Method

1   Sew   squares   together,   alternating colours, to make a rectangle 4×6 squares. Use 1cm seam allowance throughout.

2   Make paper patterns for the letters of BABY and cut them out of the coordinating fabric. Appliqué the letters to the front of the patchwork, diagonally, using zig-zag stitch and coordinating thread.

3   Place patchwork and backing fabric right sides together, then place wadding on top of patchwork. Stitch round edges through all fabrics, leaving 16cm gap in centre of one short edge. Trim all seams, turn quilt through to right side and slipstitch opening closed.

4   Stitch along all horizontal and vertical lines along edges of squares, through all thicknesses, to make quilting.

Cat Cushion

Janice Oakes, Clarksfield, Oldham, Greater Manchester

A cheeky cat dozes in a hammock amongst pretty, pastel-coloured flowers. This delightful cushion is perfect as a present for any age group – or to keep for yourself. The technique is simple, but there is clever use of contrasting fabrics, and ribbon and lace trimmings.

Materials

2 pieces 40×40cm white polyester-cotton for cushion
scraps of fabric for appliqué: plain green, yellow and two pinks in satin-type fabric; pink-and-white-patterned cotton, plus matching threads (choose fabrics of similar weights that do not fray easily)
black thread for embroidery details
3m matching pink ribbon
3m matching pink lace
polyester stuffing

Method

1   Take a piece of white fabric for front of cushion. Trace off design given (Fig 1) to make paper patterns – cat and hammock are two separate pieces, overlapping each other.
2   Cut out hammock, eyelids, inner ears, nose and soles of feet from pink satin. Cut cat from patterned cotton. Cut green satin leaves. Cut flower petals and centres from contrasting colours and fabrics to your taste.

Cut butterfly from patterned cotton.
3   Lay hammock in centre of cushion front. Place cat on hammock, with part of feet and body under hammock, and part of head and one arm over hammock, as in Fig 2. Tack in place.
4   Position ears, eyelids, nose and soles of feet, and tack. Position and tack flowers, leaves and butterfly.
5   Set machine to medium width satin stitch (zig-zag) and sew round all pieces, starting with the largest, using matching threads.
6   Embroider details of hair, eyelashes, nose, paws, navel and butterfly in black. Stitch body of butterfly in pink.
7   Stitch on ribbon 3cm from all four edges. Stitch on lace 6mm from all four edges, straight edge to the outside. Press cushion on wrong side.
8   Make two bows from remaining ribbon and attach to each end of hammock (as if holding hammock).
9   Place front and back of cushion right sides together and stitch round just over stitching line on lace, leaving opening in one side. (Take care not to catch lace in corners.) Turn through, pull out corners and press.
10   Stuff cushion and slipstitch closed with neat stitches.

Fig 1

Trace off patterns
for appliqué

Fig 2

Motif Cushion

Carol Claffey, Kendal, Cumbria

Two stuffed-felt white rabbits on a bright-red cushion (approx 30×30cm), with a basketful of embroidered multicoloured flowers – a simple design with effective use of colour.

Materials

31×36cm red hessian or linen-type fabric
2 pieces 31×36cm calico or closely woven
   fabric
62×36cm iron-on Vilene (medium weight)
106cm white ric-rac
21cm-square white felt
scrap blue felt
embroidery cottons in black, red, yellow,
   pink, blue, green, orange and brown
0.25kg white Fibrefill stuffing
white and blue sewing threads (or
   embroidery cottons if sewing by hand)

Method

1   Place hessian and one piece of calico wrong sides together and sew round all four edges.
2   Trace and cut out the two rabbits and basket to make pattern pieces. Cut each motif from Vilene, position on hessian and iron on as shown.
3   Cut motifs from felt, white for rabbits, blue for basket. Place on top of Vilene motifs and zig-zag round by machine (set for satin stitch, no 3 width and no 1 length), or chain stitch by hand. Use thread to match colour of felt.

4   Turn over and make small slits through calico in centres of rabbits and basket (taking great care). Insert small amounts of stuffing, pushing into corners with tweezers or a knitting needle. Do not overstuff. Ladder-stitch openings closed using strong or double thread.
5   Using 3 strands black embroidery cotton, stem stitch ears and mouth, satin stitch eyes, and straight stitch paws. Satin stitch flowers round mother rabbit's head using pastel green, pink, yellow and blue, filling middle of each flower with red French knot (6 strands). Fill basket with French-knot flowers of various colours (6 strands). On basket, using 3 strands of brown thread, work straight stitches vertically and horizontally. Take all threads to wrong side and finish off.
6   Cut 31×36cm Vilene to fit cushion, and iron onto calico to cover back of embroidery and slits (iron edges first). Place ric-rac on hessian, about 2.5cm from edges. Pin and stitch.
7   Place second piece of calico on hessian, right sides together, and stitch round three sides, leaving top open. Clip corners and seams, turn right sides out, push out corners and fill with Fibrefill stuffing, pushing into sides as you work up to top. Turn over top edges 1.5cm and slip stitch or ladderstitch closed, using strong or double thread and pushing in more stuffing as you go.

Position
for
flowers

Child's Neck Purse

Patricia Keen, West Drayton, Greater London

This pretty and neatly sewn purse can be made in minutes, but will make any little girl feel 'grown up'. It is about 11cm square, and could be made from scraps of fabric to match a child's outfit.

Materials

11×26cm quilted fabric
1m bias binding
15cm ribbon
75cm cord
1 press stud

Method

1 Take the quilted fabric and cut the corners of one end into gentle curves to make flap, starting 5.5cm from the end. Right sides together, machine stitch bias binding from one square corner, along one side, round the curved end and down the other side. Turn binding to wrong side, turn under and hem neatly in place. Sew short length of binding to remaining raw edge in same way.

2 Sew centre of ribbon onto right side of fabric, 3cm from curved end and about 5cm from each side. Tie ribbon in a neat bow.

3 Turn up straight end to about 6cm from the curved end, and ladderstitch each side to form the bag.

4 Tie knots at each end of the cord and sew them onto the sides of bag, under the flap, with ends hidden inside the bag. Sew on press stud to fasten flap just underneath bow.

Little Red Riding Hood Play Cushion

Valerie Smith, Salt, Stafford

A colourful play cushion with five finger puppets: Little Red Riding Hood, her Mother, Grandmother, the Woodcutter and the Wolf. It is simply made from washable quilted fabrics, and measures approximately 45cm square. This clever idea could be adapted to any favourite fairy tale or story. Illustrated on book jacket.

Materials

2 pieces 50×50cm green polyester-cotton fabric
2 pieces 50×50cm wadding
2 pieces 50×50cm nylon lining
25×12.5cm checked quilted fabric for Red Riding Hood's house
small pieces quilted fabric in red, blue and dark green
20×12.5cm checked quilted fabric for Grandmother's house
small pieces yellow cotton fabric for footpath
small pieces Vilene interfacing for footpath
50cm green nylon zip
45cm square cushion
matching sewing threads
pieces of green, red, blue and checked quilted fabric for 'people' puppets
scraps of cream polyester and iron-on Vilene for faces
scraps of brown, black, yellow and red felt
scraps of brown leather for handbag and axe
scrap of cream lace for Grandmother
piece of brown acrylic fleece for Wolf
scrap of stuffing for Wolf
red, blue and white embroidery thread

Method

To make the cushion cover, place one piece of green polyester-cotton wrong side up, put a square of wadding on top, then a square of lining. Tack all three layers together. Repeat with the other three pieces to make the back. On back only, sew three parallel lines from side to side, 12.5cm apart. Put the back to one side.

RED RIDING HOOD'S HOUSE (top left)

1 Take the checked quilted fabric and cut out 2 window holes, each 5cm wide by 3.5cm high. They should be 3.5cm from the sides of the house and 5cm from the bottom. Slit the corners of each hole, turn the edges under and hem. Cut 2 pieces of dark-green fabric 6×7cm for the windows.

2 Turn in the sides and bottom of the house and sew it onto the front of the cushion, about 5cm from the left side and 10cm from the top (do not sew down top of house). Place the green windows inside the holes so that they are about 1cm from the bottom of the house. Sew down the tops and sides of the windows, through all 3 fabrics, leaving bottom edge open to form pocket.

3 Cut roof from blue quilted fabric according to the pattern. Turn in edges and sew onto cushion, overlapping slightly onto the house.

4 Cut 9×6cm red quilted fabric for the door, turn in edges and sew on between the windows.

GRANDMOTHER'S HOUSE (bottom right)

1 Take second piece of checked quilted fabric and cut out one window hole as before, but on the left side only. Cut dark-green window as before.

2 Sew house onto cushion as before, 6cm from right side of cushion and 5cm from bottom. Sew in window as before.

3 Cut roof from red quilted material using smaller pattern and sew on as before.

4 Cut and sew door as before, but in blue.

WOODCUTTER'S HUT

1 Cut out from dark-green quilted fabric, using pattern given. Turn in edges and sew onto cushion about 7.5cm from left side and 9cm from bottom.

2 Cut 11×7.5cm dark-green quilted fabric. Turn under and machine top edge (which is to be left open). Turn under remaining edges and sew onto cushion, overlapping bottom of first piece by 3.5cm. To make the pocket, sew 2 vertical lines down second piece, 3.5cm from each side.

THE WOLF'S TREES (top right)

1 Cut a 12.5cm square from dark-green quilted fabric. Turn in the edges and one corner, and arrange on cushion with flattened corner at the base. Sew onto cushion, leaving a 5cm opening in top left edge for pocket. Stitch diagonally through 'tree' from centre of top right edge to centre of bottom left edge, to form base of pocket.

2 Cut a 7.5cm square from dark-green quilted fabric. Turn in edges, flatten one corner and arrange as before, overlapping bottom right edge of larger tree. Sew onto cushion.

FOOTPATH

Cut 7 paving stones from yellow cotton using pattern, and 7 pieces of Vilene slightly smaller. Turn in cotton edges over the Vilene, tack, then sew to cushion to make footpath. Remove tacking.

TO MAKE UP CUSHION

Place back and front of cushion cover together and sew zip onto bottom edge. Turn right sides together and sew round remaining 3 sides. Remove tacking and turn right sides out. Place cushion inside completed cover.

TO MAKE PUPPETS

1 Cut 2 of basic pattern for each of the 5 puppets: Little Red Riding Hood in red quilted fabric, Mother in green, Grandmother in blue, the Woodcutter in check and the Wolf in brown acrylic fleece.

2 For all except the Wolf, cut 2 arms. Fold arm in half, right sides out. Turn under the edges of the rounded end and long seam and oversew, leaving remaining end open.

3 With right sides together, pin together back and front of puppet, tucking in the arms as indicated on pattern. Sew round top and sides, 7mm from the edge, sewing in arms. Turn right sides out and hem bottom.

4 Cut face from cream polyester using pattern. Back with iron-on Vilene. Cut small circles of black felt for eyes and sew on with stitch of white embroidery thread in centre. Embroider mouth with red. Oversew face to puppet as marked on pattern.

LITTLE RED RIDING HOOD

Using embroidery thread, sew three French

Play Cushion Patterns

All the patterns are actual sizes, and seams are allowed.

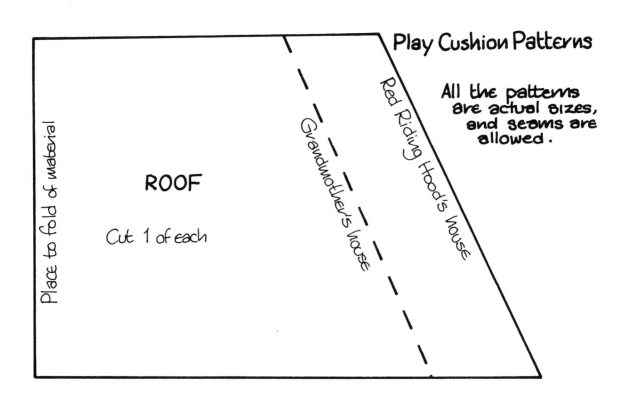

ROOF

Cut 1 of each

Place to fold of material

Grandmother's house

Red Riding Hood's house

STEPS ON FOOTPATH

fabric

vilene

Cut 7 of each

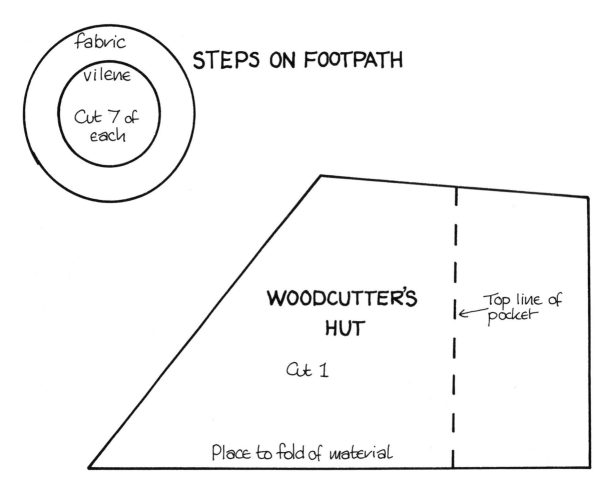

WOODCUTTER'S HUT

Cut 1

← Top line of pocket

Place to fold of material

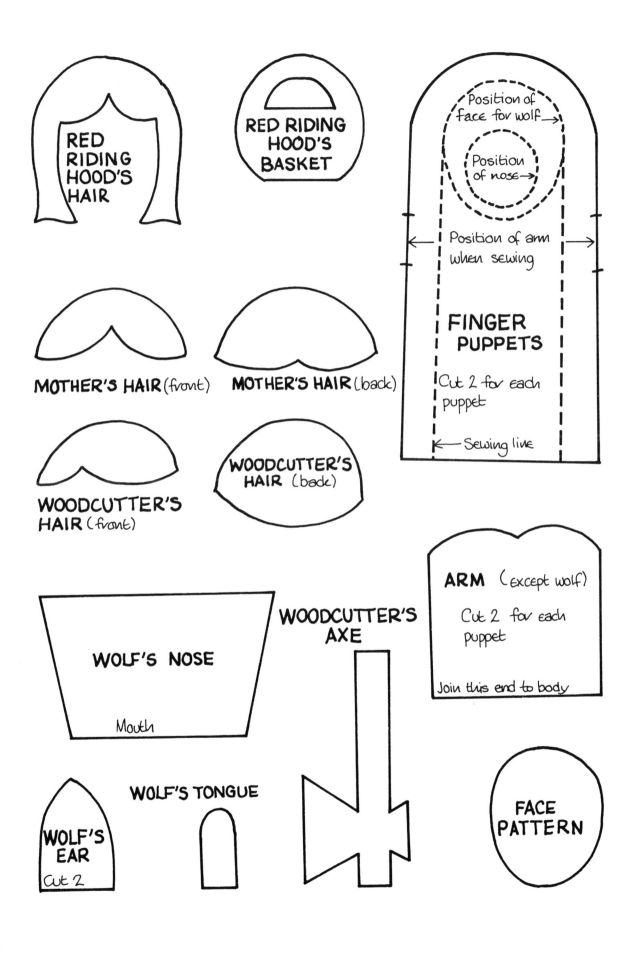

RED RIDING HOOD'S HAIR

RED RIDING HOOD'S BASKET

Position of face for wolf →

Position of nose →

Position of arm when sewing

FINGER PUPPETS

Cut 2 for each puppet

← Sewing line

MOTHER'S HAIR (front)

MOTHER'S HAIR (back)

WOODCUTTER'S HAIR (front)

WOODCUTTER'S HAIR (back)

WOLF'S NOSE

Mouth

WOODCUTTER'S AXE

ARM (except wolf)

Cut 2 for each puppet

Join this end to body

WOLF'S TONGUE

WOLF'S EAR

Cut 2

FACE PATTERN

knots down front of body for buttons. Cut hair from yellow felt using pattern and oversew top of hair in place on body. Cut out the basket from brown leather using pattern and sew onto arm.

MOTHER
Using embroidery threads, sew several French knots to front of body to form coloured pattern. Cut hair from brown felt using pattern and oversew in place.

GRANDMOTHER
Take a piece of lace about 15cm long, join edges and gather at the top edge to make round cap. Stitch centre of cap to top of head and make a row of stitching around head to complete mob cap. Gather a small piece of lace and stitch to puppet under face.

WOODCUTTER
Cut hair from brown felt using pattern and oversew to top of head. Sew on a tiny piece of brown felt above mouth for moustache. Cut axe from brown leather using pattern and stitch to arm.

WOLF
Cut nose from brown fleece and tongue from red felt using patterns. Sew sides of nose together and turn through. Place seam down, turn mouth edges under (narrow end), insert tongue and ladderstitch to close. Embroider mouth in dark-brown zig-zag. Stuff nose and ladderstitch to puppet. Make black-felt eyes as before. Cut ears from brown felt and sew on, gathering slightly. Place puppets in their pockets and the cushion is ready for play.

Patchwork

colour photograph on pages 82/83

Owl cushion cover   70
Hexagon patchwork cushion   71
Petal cushion   72
Needlecase and pincushion   76
Tote bag   78
Commemorative cushion   86
Cathedral window patchwork evening bag   90
Cathedral window patchwork needlecase   93

Owl Cushion Cover

Sally Barras, Wednesfield, Wolverhampton, West Midlands

This wise patchwork owl would make a striking conversation piece for any sofa – or he could be appliquéd to a bag. The cushion cover measures approximately 40cm square.

Materials

tracing paper

strong, thin paper to make patterns

scraps of fabric in blue, dark brown and light brown

2 pieces 40cm square dark-brown fabric for cushion cover

scraps of felt in grey and black for eyes; yellow for beak and feet; white (or yellow) for moon

matching sewing threads

Method

1 Enlarge design and trace onto paper, using a ruler to obtain straight lines, omitting eyes, beak, feet and moon. Number and label each piece carefully (30 pieces in all). Cut out all the pieces.

2 Place all pieces labelled blue onto wrong

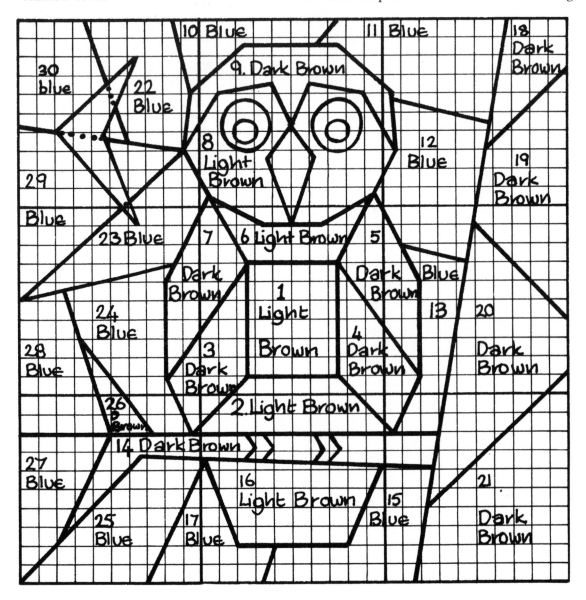

70

side of blue fabric. Pin and cut round each piece, leaving paper. Arrange blue pieces on right side of one dark-brown square, following the design and leaving a little of the brown backing square showing all round for seam allowance. Tack each blue piece in position, removing paper pattern first. Machine or hand appliqué the edges of each blue piece.

3   Pin remaining pattern pieces onto wrong side of appropriate fabric. Cut each piece, leaving 1cm margin all round. Turn edges over pattern and tack in place, taking care to fold in corners without distorting original shape.

4   Following original pattern, oversew pieces together on the wrong side in correct position. Press on wrong side, remove tacking and paper, then press again to give sharp creases.

5   Hand stitch owl and tree in place to blue sky and backing square.

6   Cut felt pieces for eyes, beak, feet and moon. Stitch in place.

7   Place the brown squares right sides together and stitch round three sides, just to edge of patchwork. Turn through and press, pressing turnings on fourth side (this will be slipstitched closed when cushion pad is in place).

Hexagon Cushion

M. Ramsey, Leicester

Traditional hexagon patchwork has been used to make this 46cm cushion. The technique is simple, but the neatness and careful choice of fabrics make it very successful. Choose contrasting plain and patterned materials in toning colours for best effect, and use one of the fabrics for the back.

Materials

76mm metal hexagon template
thick paper or card to make 37 patches
scraps of 3 fabrics, patterned and plain
1.75m piping cord
scrap of one of patchwork fabrics to cover
  piping cord (cut on bias)
0.5m fabric for lining
0.5m of one of patchwork fabrics for back of
  cushion
36cm zip
36cm feather cushion pad

Method

1   Use metal template to cut 37 patches from paper or card. Cut fabric patches round paper ones, making them a little bigger for turnings. Cut 19 from first fabric (1 for centre, 18 for outside ring); 12 from second fabric for next ring in; 6 from third fabric for inner ring. Think carefully about where to use each fabric. Always cut on straight grain of fabric.

2   Tack each fabric patch securely over a card template. Assemble into place on table to check design. Sew patches together with small neat stitches in matching thread.

3   When all patches are sewn together, turn part of outer patches over to give an even, approximately hexagonal edge to cushion. Cover piping cord with fabric and hem neatly to edge of cushion.

4   Remove paper templates from all patches. Cut lining to fit whole of patchwork, turn under outside edge, and hem neatly in place over back of patchwork, stitching on top of piping fabric.

5   Zip is across centre of cushion back, so cut the back in two equal halves, allowing extra for turnings round outside and along zip edges. Hem zip edges and insert zip. Slipstitch back pieces together where zip does not reach edge. Hem back to patchwork, as close to piping cord as possible. Insert cushion.

Petal Cushion

M. Wilson, Barnt Green, Birmingham

This pretty cushion (35.5cm in diameter) is made of separate patchwork petals, each lightly stuffed to give a raised effect like a real flower. You could use any colour combination, but make sure the shades complement each other as well as the browns and pinks shown.

Materials

0.5m cotton curtain lining or muslin for backing
0.5m cotton fabric in each of 5 toning shades
small amount terylene stuffing (as used for quilting)
35.5cm (14in) cushion pad
4 Velcro spot-ons or press studs
matching threads

Method

1   Cut out paper patterns: 280mm diameter circle, 355mm diameter circle, and one each of petal shapes in Fig 1.

2   Cut a 280mm circle from the backing material and mark into 8 equal segments using basting thread or tailor's chalk.

3   Choose the colour that is to be the centre and outside of the flower (colour A) and cut four 76mm squares. Fold each in half, wrong sides together, then bring corners of folded edge down to the centre of open edge to form a triangle (Fig 2). Pin triangles, folded sides up, in centre of backing circle, in line with marked segments, apexes together (Fig 3). Sew in place with a few stitches in the corners of each triangle.

4   Take fabric colour B, fold in half, right sides together. Using smallest petal pattern, mark 8 petals. Baste round edges of rectangle to hold two layers in place, then machine round marked outside lines of petals, leaving 50mm opening at pointed ends for turning through. Cut out petals and turn through. Press. Stuff each petal very lightly and machine closed (these ends will not be visible).

5   Arrange petals on backing circle, over-lapping triangles as shown (Fig 4), with the centre of each petal along a marked line. Attach petals by slip hemming the sides only, up to where they touch one another. Do not sew down rounded tips. Use matching thread.

6   Repeat 5 with colour C, using the medium-sized petal shape. Place these petals immediately on top of the first ones, but about 25mm further out. Attach as before.

7   Repeat 5 with colour D, using the largest petal shape. Position these in between the marked lines so that their centres are over the overlapping edges of the previous rings of petals, again 25mm further out. If the final petals come over the edge of the backing circle, trim them to fit.

8   Mark out a 355mm circle on colour A, then allow another 10mm for turnings. Cut out circle. Cut from this a 260mm circle, to form a ring. Neaten both raw edges of ring. Turn inner edge under and place ring on top of circle of petals, aligning with edge of backing circle (ring right side up). Top-stitch ring to petal circle to form an outer border.

9   Cut out another 355mm circle with 10mm turning allowance, on colour E. Neaten raw edge. Place on petal circle, right sides together, and machine round edge, leaving 280mm opening. Press seam and attach fasteners to opening. Insert cushion pad.

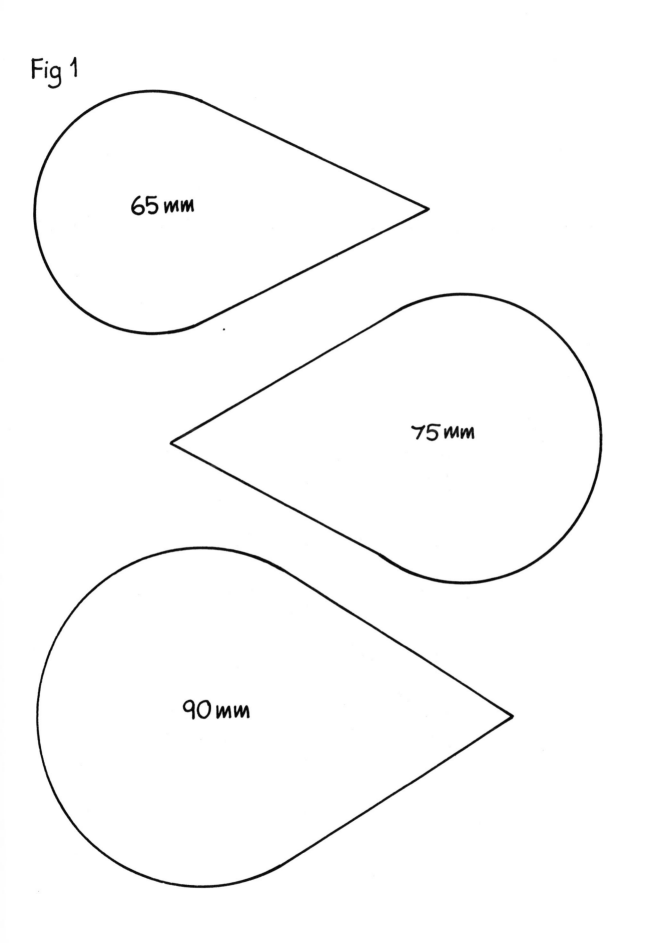

Fig 1

65 mm

75 mm

90 mm

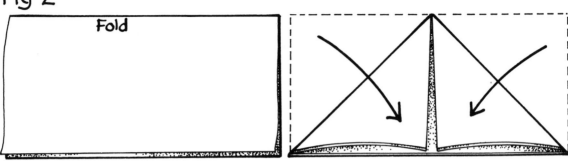

Fig 2

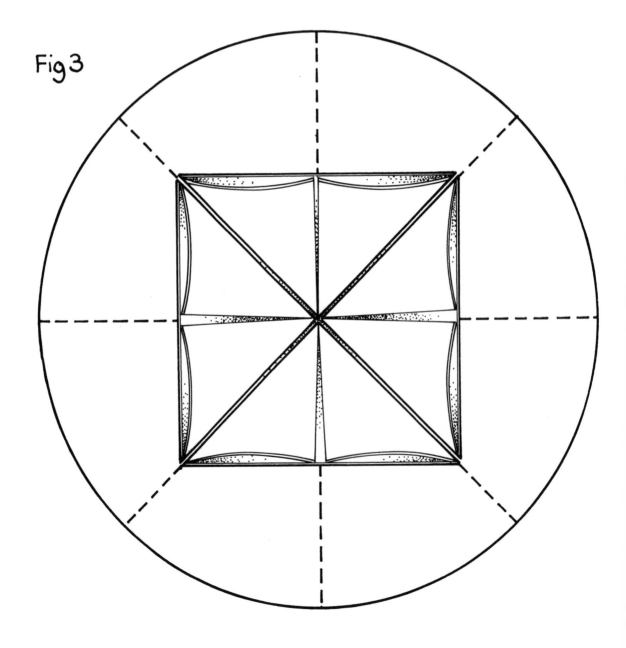

Fig 3

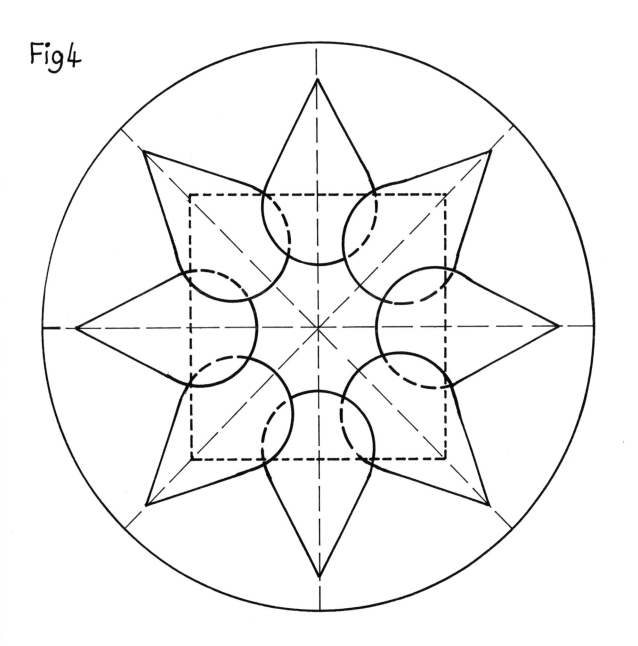

Fig 4

Needlecase and Pincushion

Diana Newman, Battersea, London

This pretty matching pair of needlecase and pincushion would make an ideal gift. The log-cabin patchwork looks much more complicated than it really is, though it must be neatly done, especially on this small scale (about 10 and 13cm square, respectively). Choose bright contrasting coloured fabrics, with very small patterns.

Needlecase materials

115×115mm calico for backing
25×25mm cotton fabric for centre square, contrasting with other patchwork fabrics
4 strips 25×230mm cotton fabric, each in contrasting colour for patchwork
115×115mm contrasting cotton fabric for back of case
115×75mm cotton fabric for pocket
115×230mm cotton fabric for inside of case
115×230mm terylene wadding

scraps of cord
2 wooden beads
matching threads

Method

1   Fold calico square in half then half again to find centre. Make diagonal marks from corner to corner as guides to keeping the patchwork even. Place small square of cotton fabric in centre of calico, wrong side down, and pin (Fig 1).

2   Start adding strips in the order shown in the diagram (Fig 2), cutting lengths from the strips to fit as you work. Place the strip right side down, machine as shown (use the same seam allowance throughout), fold over and press. Machine through the calico and take care to keep the pieces straight. Build each side of the square in one of the four colours, contrasting light and dark. The needlecase shown uses red, yellow, green and white, in that order.

3   Place finished patchwork square with cotton back, right sides together, and sew down one side. Press seam open (Fig 3).

4   Sew 5mm seam along one long edge of the pocket. Tack to one end of lining, wrong sides together.

5   Place lining on top of wadding, pocket uppermost. Cut 2 pieces of cord and lay

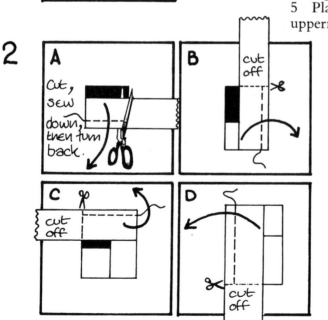

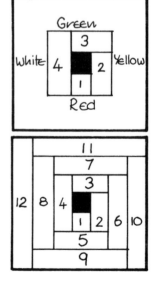

76

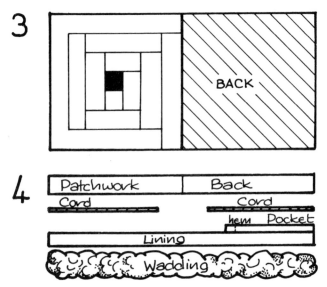

3

BACK

4

Patchwork | Back
Cord | Cord
hem | Pocket
Lining
Wadding

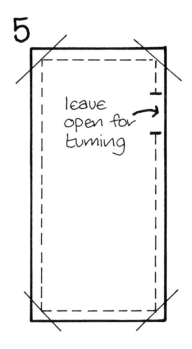

5

leave open for turning

them on top, slightly overlapping the ends of the lining. Place patchwork and back on top of cords, with back over pocket (Fig 4). Stitch round all four edges, through all layers (5mm seam allowance), leaving a small gap for turning. Clip corners, turn through and slipstitch opening (Fig 5).

6 Attach beads to cords with small knots. Press.

Pincushion materials

180×180mm calico
scraps of red, yellow, blue, green cotton for patchwork, and white for centre square
scrap of kapok stuffing
matching thread
matching embroidery thread
4 wooden beads

Method

1 Follow instructions for needlecase, making up a log-cabin square until the patchwork measures 180×180mm. Press well.
2 Fold in half, right sides together. Sew ends, stopping 5mm from open edge (Fig 1).
3 Pull apart the open edges and place tops of seamed edges together, making a square with diagonal seams. Stitch the open seam, leaving gap for turning (Fig 2).
4 Turn right sides out, stuff firmly and slipstitch opening.
5 Sew a length of embroidery thread on each corner, thread on a bead and tie a large knot immediately behind it.

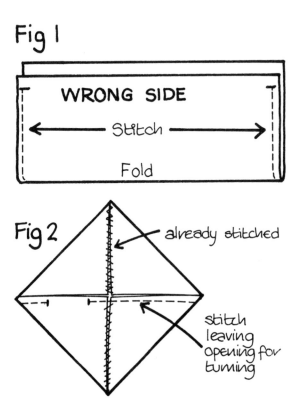

Fig 1

WRONG SIDE

Stitch

Fold

Fig 2

already stitched

stitch leaving opening for turning

Tote Bag

K. Elson, Westcliff-on-Sea, Essex

Eyecatching results can be achieved with a bold patchwork design and strong colour contrast, as in this cheerful tote bag (about 33×39cm). It would certainly brighten up any shopping day, could carry a teenager's school books, and would make an ideal knitting bag. Use a strong cotton such as twill, sailcloth or denim, and avoid any fabric that frays easily.

Materials

thin card for template (cereal packet will do)
30cm light-coloured strong cotton (90cm wide)
30cm dark-coloured strong cotton (90cm wide)
scrap of contrasting, brightly coloured strong cotton for centre

Method

1 Using compasses, draw a 28cm diameter circle onto the card. Keeping compass set to same radius, place its point on the circle and make a pencil mark on the circle. Place point of compass on this mark and make another mark on the circle, continuing until you have marked out the six corners of a hexagon. Draw a line to divide the hexagon in half (see Fig 1). Leave one half plain. On the other half, draw lines from the corners to the centre of the hexagon, to give four radial lines in all. On each of these lines, draw points 4.5cm and 8.5cm from the corner. Join up these points as shown to make the patchwork pattern. Cut out the plain half of hexagon. On the other half, cut along the lines parallel with the outside edge, to make the three pattern pieces.

2 Cut 2 pieces 35.5×26cm from dark fabric for top half of bag. Cut 2 pieces 35.5×20cm from light fabric for bottom of bag. Cut 2 pieces 30×6.5cm from light fabric for handles.

3 Place together one top and one bottom piece, right sides together, with centre edges (ie the longest) touching. Place the half-hexagon template in the middle 6mm from the centre edge, and mark around the template (Fig 2). Remove template and cut 6mm inside the mark to allow for turnings. Make sure you cut in exactly the same place on each piece, to match pattern.

4 Cut hexagon strips: 1 large strip each in light and dark fabric; 1 medium strip each in light and dark fabric; 2 centre pieces in the third colour. Allow 6mm extra all round on all pieces for seam allowances.

5 Stay stitch (long machine stitch) all inside corners of strips and bag pieces to reinforce (Fig 3). Snip into these corners. Join hexagon strips together as in Fig 4. To avoid tucks at corners, machine with snipped corners uppermost, sewing right into corners, then lifting machine foot with needle still in fabric, and turning work round while pushing surplus fabric away from you. Stitch all seams twice for strength. Neaten seams and press.

6 To join top and bottom of bag, match strips carefully, right sides together, pinning along seams of pattern for accuracy. Stitch centre seam with pins in place, with 6mm seam allowance.

7 Sew together the two back pieces of bag. Place back and front right sides together and sew side and bottom seams (6mm seams throughout).

8 Turn over top edge 6mm, then another 25mm, press and machine hem. Fold handles lengthwise, right sides together, stitch down long edge and one end. Turn through and press. Turn in and oversew other end. Place ends on (and level with) hem, 7.5cm apart. Stitch in a square, then diagonally for extra strength. Press.

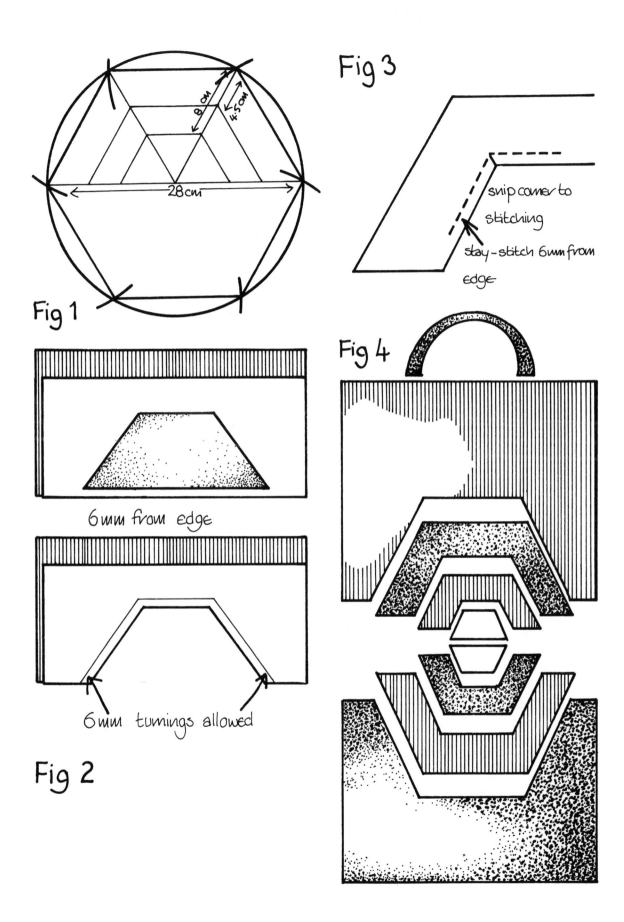

Fig 3

Fig 1

8 cm

4·5 cm

28 cm

snip corner to

stitching

stay-stitch 6mm from

edge

6 mm from edge

6 mm turnings allowed

Fig 2

Fig 4

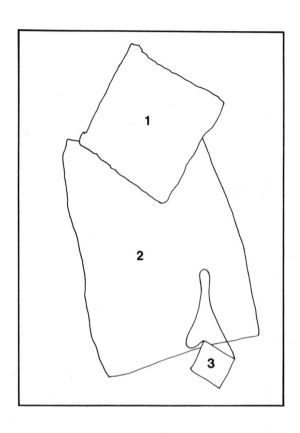

APPLIQUÉ AND QUILTING (opposite)
1 Cat cushion (page 59)
2 Baby's quilt (page 58)
3 Child's neck purse (page 64)

PATCHWORK (overleaf)
1 Commemorative cushion (page 86)
2 Tote bag (page 78)
3 Hexagon patchwork cushion (page 71)
4 Petal cushion (page 72)
5 Cathedral window patchwork evening bag (page 90)
6 Needlecase and pincushion (page 76)
7 Cathedral window patchwork needlecase (page 93)
8 Owl cushion cover (page 70)

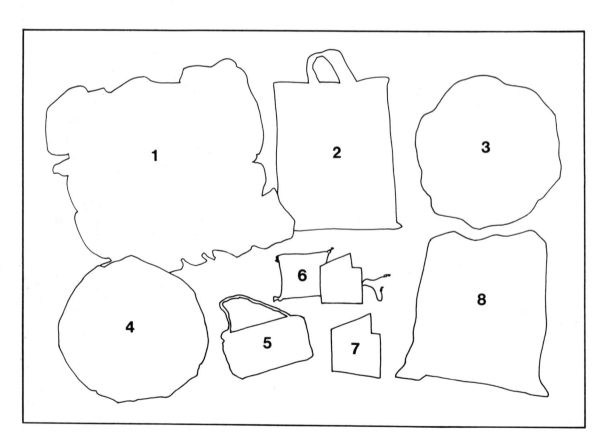

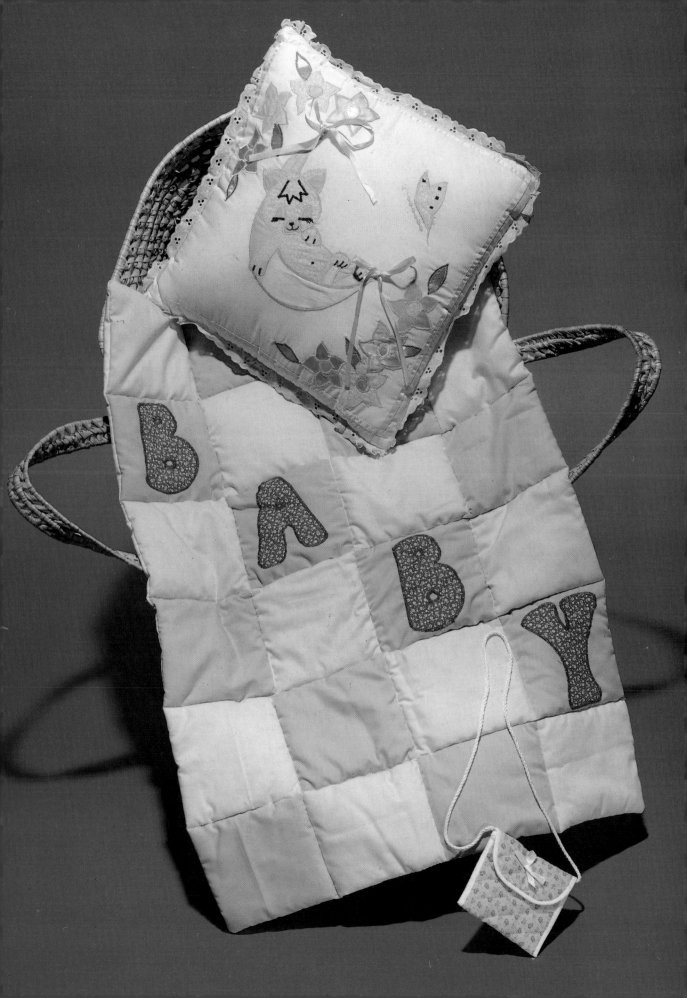

SEWING AND EMBROIDERY *(opposite)*

1 Toddler's hooded top *(page 97)*
2 Embroidered robin Christmas card *(page 96)*
3 Tapestry panel *(page 99)*
4 Reversible play cloak – also shown on page 118 *(page 105)*
5 Nursery picture – Goosey Goosey Gander *(page 108)*

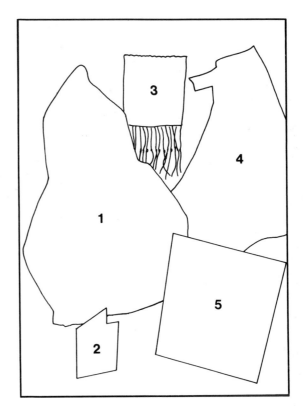

Commemorative Cushion

Nicky Chandler, St Leonard's, Exeter, Devon

This delightful cushion can be made to com-
memorate a birth, christening, engagement,
golden wedding anniversary, or, as here, a
wedding day. Ideally, you should follow the
wedding's colour scheme, using scraps of the
bridesmaids' dress fabric. The cushion measures
approximately 60cm square (including frill).

Materials

20×20cm evenweave fabric for embroidery
  (12 threads to 1cm)
embroidery silk in three tones of chosen
  colour (here pink), plus green and yellow
1m plain pink fabric (90cm wide)
scraps of pink-and-white fabric
scraps of toning multicoloured fabric
54×54cm white cotton lining
40.5cm zip
cushion pad approx 50cm square

Method

CROSS STITCH PANEL

1 Using squared paper and the alphabet
plan (Fig 1), design your lettering according
to the occasion. There should be one square
space between letters, and two squares
between words. Find the centres of the lines
and align them. Draw each line of letters
within a box, with each letter fitting carefully within the box. Copy the flower design
on both sides to complete the plan (Fig 2).
2 On the evenweave fabric, tack a
16×16cm square, following line of weave.
Fold in half, open, and tack up fold line.
Repeat, opposite way, so that lines of
tacking cross at centre of square.
3 Transfer design to fabric, starting at the
centre (each square on paper represents two
threads on fabric).
4 Work the cross stich, following colour
scheme on plan.

TO MAKE UP CUSHION

1 From the plain fabric, cut a 55cm square
(for cushion back); 24 triangles (half squares)
using given template (Fig 3); strips of fabric
10cm wide, totalling 4m (for frill). Cutting
plan for 90cm fabric is shown in Fig 4.
2 Cut 20 triangles from pink-and-white
fabric, and 20 triangles from multicoloured
fabric.
3 Using the patchwork plan, make up
cushion front (1cm seams throughout).
First, sew all diagonal seams to make 32
squares; then sew these into the 6 rows (the 2
middle rows split into halves). Next, join
together the top 2 rows, the bottom 2 rows
and the middle 2 rows (still in halves). This
should give 4 pieces of patchwork (Fig 5).
4 Trim embroidered square, leaving 1cm
seam allowance all round tacking. Sew
square in place in patchwork, stitching along
line of weave. Sew all remaining patchwork
seams, using 1cm seam allowance throughout. Trim corners, press and tack lining to
back of patchwork.
5 Join all 10cm strips to make frill, using
French seams. Hem one long edge. Gather
other long edge, using 2 rows of long
machine stitches, 3mm and 1cm from edge.
Mark frill into 4 sections using pins. Attach
frill to cushion, right sides together, with a
pin in centre of each side of cushion. Stitch
1cm from edge.
6 Zip is inserted to one side of cushion
back. Cut back in two, 12cm from one edge.
Press one edge under 1cm and stitch in one
side of zip, stitching close to teeth. Press
other edge under 1.5cm, tack edge to
machine stitching and stitch close to teeth on
other side of zip. This covers zip. Remove
tacking and make small seams at ends of zip.
7 Trim back to size of cushion front. Place
back over top of frill, right sides of cushion
together. Stitch round all edges (1cm seam),
leaving zip slightly open to turn through.
Trim seam, clip corners, neaten by zig-
zagging, and remove all tacking. Turn
through and insert cushion.

Fig 1

Alphabet and Numbers

Fig 2

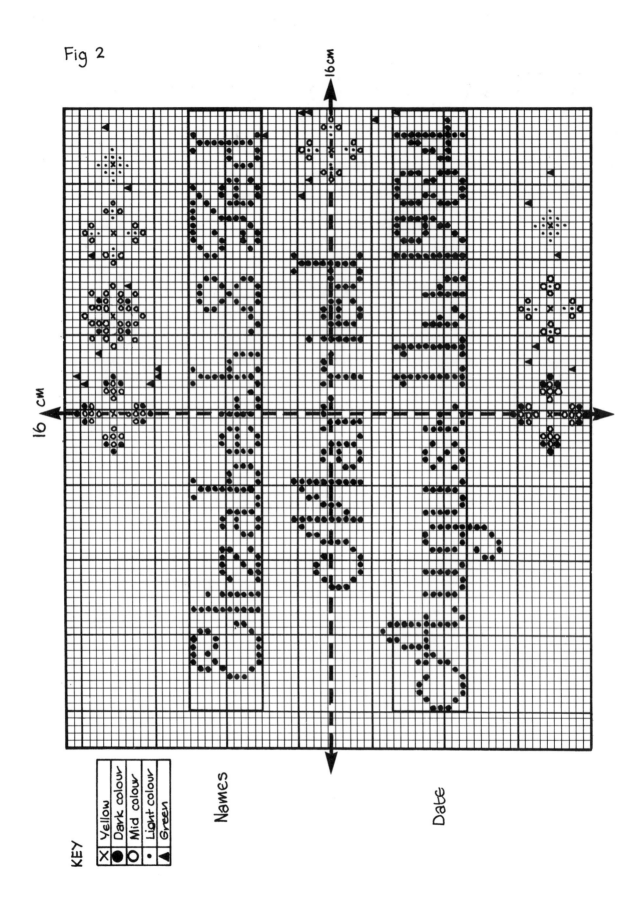

16cm

16 cm

KEY

X	Yellow
●	Dark colour
O	Mid colour
·	Light colour
▲	Green

Names

Date

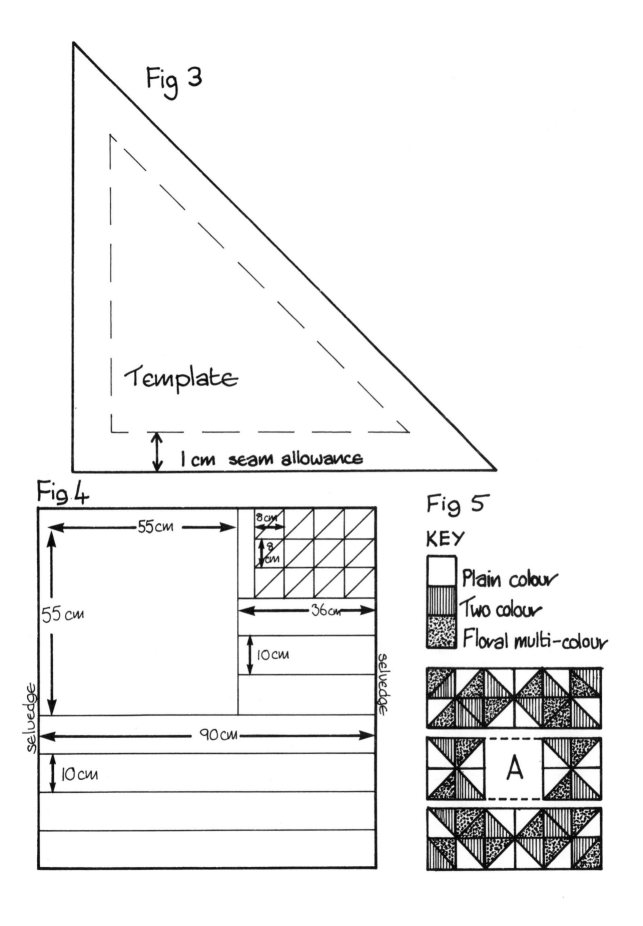

Fig 3

Template

↕ 1 cm seam allowance

Fig 4

← 55 cm →

55 cm

selvedge

90 cm

10 cm

8 cm

8 cm

← 36 cm →

10 cm

selvedge

Fig 5

KEY

Plain colour

Two colour

Floral multi-colour

A

Cathedral Window Patchwork Evening Bag

Bette Bell, Lostoch Hall, Preston, Lancashire

This pretty evening bag (approx 18×10cm) needs care and patience, but the results are ample reward, and would make a really original gift. Silk fabric gives a luxurious feel but is more difficult to work with – fine cotton would work equally well.

Materials

9cm square template in light card
50cm fine cream-coloured cotton or silk
water erasable pen
67 small squares, approx 3cm, of fine cotton or silk in various 'jewel' colours
approx 33×40cm heavy Vilene (preferably pelmet-weight)
approx 33×40cm matching fabric for lining
3 strips matching fabric, 1m×2cm, for plaited strap (cut on cross-grain)
small, pretty button
matching threads

Method

1 Cut 32 squares of cream-coloured fabric, each 10cm square exactly, and cut on the straight grain. They must be exactly the same.

2 Place template in centre of one square and press over 5mm turnings all round, keeping grain absolutely straight. Remove template.

3 Mark centre of square and fold in half (turnings inside), matching points (a) to (b), and (c) to (d) (see Figs 1 and 2). Oversew edges from fold to halfway along, taking the minimum amount of fabric. Open square and refold, matching (a) to (c) and (b) to (d). Oversew as before from fold to halfway along.

4 Smooth piece down to lie flat, with corners meeting at centre. Join these corners with a cross stitch. Bring outside corners to the centre and hold with another cross stitch, but leave diagonals unstitched this time (see Figs 3a and 3b). These open diagonals are on the bias, which is important later. Smooth down, without pressing. Repeat stages 2–4 for all 32 squares, checking that they are exactly the same size, and on the straight grain.

5 Join 4 squares together in a row as shown in Fig 4, oversewing edges with smooth sides of squares facing. These stitches will be hidden later. Make 7 rows in this way, each of 4 squares.

6 Join these rows to make body of bag, adding remaining 4 squares to make sides exactly as shown in Fig 5. Leave flat for next stage.

7 Coloured fabric squares are to fit into the squares bounded by the bias diagonals. Cut 67 squares so that they just fit inside the diagonals (see Fig 6). Pin or tack in place (leaving the half squares on the outside edges till later).

8 Roll bias diagonals over edges of coloured squares, making even, matching curves, and stabstitch or hem in place very neatly. As you reach a corner, roll over the next side and stitch across both hems with 2 tiny stitches.

9 Make up bag by joining side seams, joining B to C, and A to D (see Fig 5). Sew on coloured squares as before to cover seams.

10 Fold under the corners of front flap (see Fig 5). Where there are half squares left at edges of bag, attach 2 sides of a coloured square, then fold remaining half over to back and catch down with a few stitches.

11 Cut a piece of Vilene slightly smaller than body of bag, then cut 2 side pieces separately (also slightly smaller). Cut the same pieces from lining fabric, but 5mm bigger than bag all round to allow for turnings. Tack Vilene to wrong side of lining. Machine stitch along fold lines to help fold Vilene. Stitch lining seams, turn under edges and slipstitch neatly into bag, leaving gaps to insert strap between bag and lining at sides.

12 Fold strips in half lengthwise, right sides together, stitch, turn through and press. Plait strips together to make strap to length required. Insert at sides of bag, between lining and bag, and stitch firmly in place.

13 Stitch button to centre of front and work thread loop on flap to fasten.

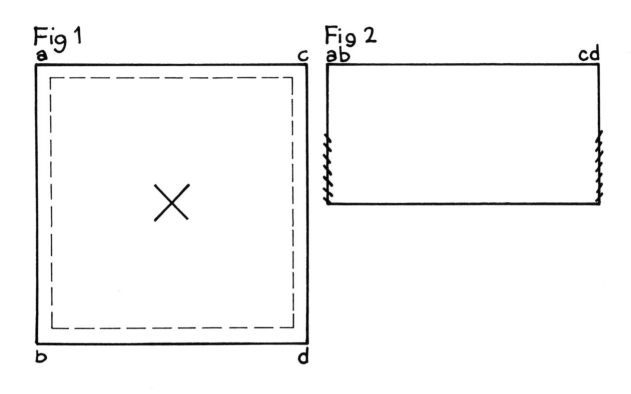

Fig 1

a   c

X

b   d

Fig 2

ab   cd

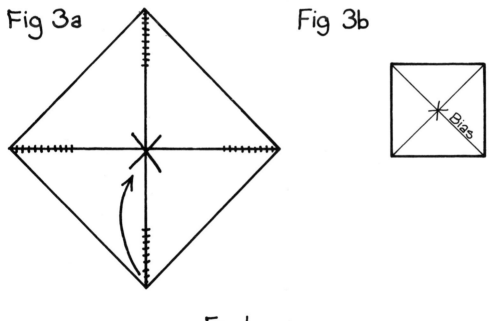

Fig 3a

Fig 3b

Bias

Fig 4

Fig 5

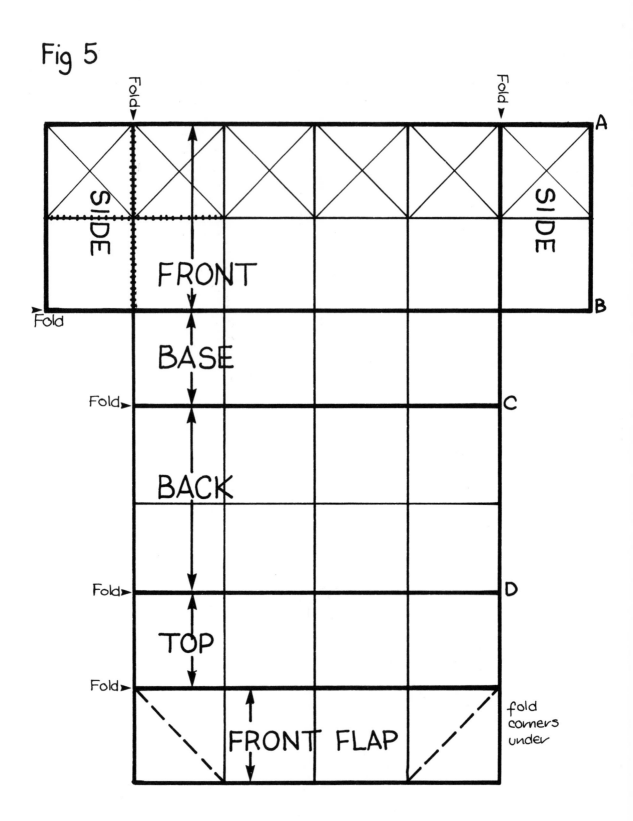

Fig 6

Fig 6

Front

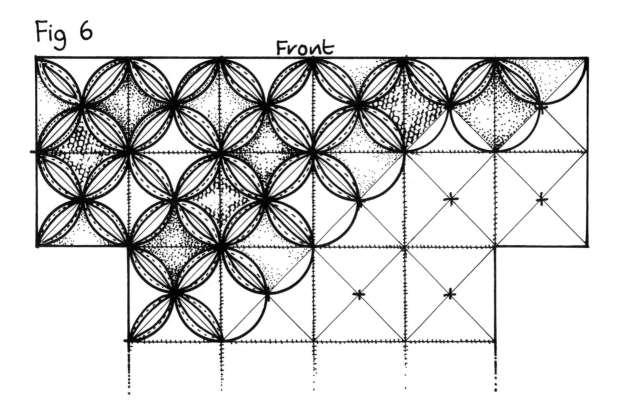

Cathedral Window Patchwork Needlecase

Sheena Blake, Chilwell, Nottingham

An attractive and practical present that is much easier to make than it looks, although it does require neat working. The patterned fabric should be chosen to tone with the plain to make the most effective use of this patchwork pattern.

Materials

2 pieces plain fabric, 230mm square
1 piece printed fabric, 216×115mm
4 pieces same printed fabric, 63.5mm square
1 piece same printed fabric, 77×20mm
1 piece pelmet Vilene 204×102mm
One 16mm button
2 pieces felt, 204×102mm

Method

1   Fold one square of plain fabric in half, right sides together, and seam short ends.
2   Open top and bring seams together. Seam A to B and C to D (Fig 1) and turn right side out.

Fig 1

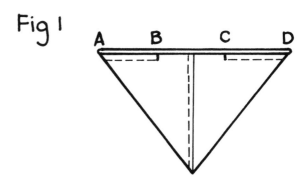

Fig 2

Fig 3

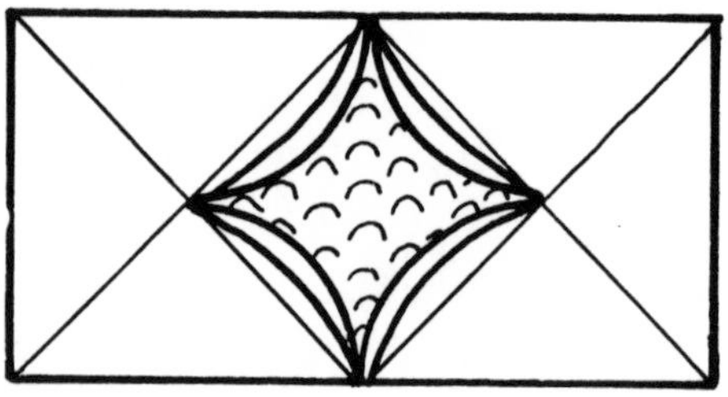

Fig 4

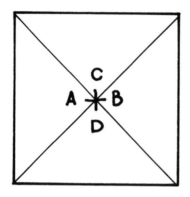

3 Flatten, pushing the corners out, and close the opening with small stitches. The seams should lie flat.

4 Fold each corner to the centre of the patch, pin and sew the corners down with small stitches, A to B and C to D (Fig 2).

5 Repeat steps 1–4 with second square of plain fabric. Then place the patches together and topstitch along one side.

6 Open out, right side up, and pin one 63.5mm square in the centre 'square' of the patchwork. Then turn and hem each side of the 'square' over the patterned fabric (Fig 3).

7 Cut the remaining three 63.5mm squares into triangles, place one in each triangle of the patchwork and hem as centre square. Turn in a 1.6mm hem on the outside edge (Fig 4). This completes the patchwork.

8 To make lining cover the pelmet Vilene with the 216×115mm piece of printed fabric and place on the wrong side of the patchwork. Sew the lining firmly to the patchwork, inserting small loop made with 77×20mm piece printed fabric in middle of one short edge.

9 Attach button opposite loop on right side of the patchwork.

10 Pink edges of felt and sew them to the case with a few stitches in the centre through the lining (but not through the patchwork).

Sewing and Embroidery

colour photographs on pages 84 and 118/119

Embroidered robin Christmas card   96

Toddler's hooded top   97

Embroidered greetings cards   98

Tapestry panel   99

Reversible play cloak   105

Nursery picture – Goosey Goosey Gander   108

Strawberry workbox   110

Decorative handbag   113

Party bag   114

Applied embroidered fabric picture   122

Full-fringed tablecloth and napkins   124

Embroidered Robin Christmas Card

D. King, Clevedon, Avon

A cheap and simple way to make sure your Christmas cards are totally original. This jolly robin is embroidered onto fabric, then stuck onto a piece of card. You could design your own card, and extend the idea to any greetings card – or make a set of notelets as a gift.

Materials

8×11cm white Binca cloth or other even-weave fabric (5 holes to 1cm)
embroidery thread in red, brown, grey and green (use 3 strands)

16×21cm gold-coloured card, or card pre-folded to 10×15cm
glue

Method

1 Following the chart, embroider the robin in cross stitch. Trim edges.
2 Stick robin onto card, using a small amount of glue at each corner.
Note: The alternative snowman design should be embroidered and then stuck onto coloured card.

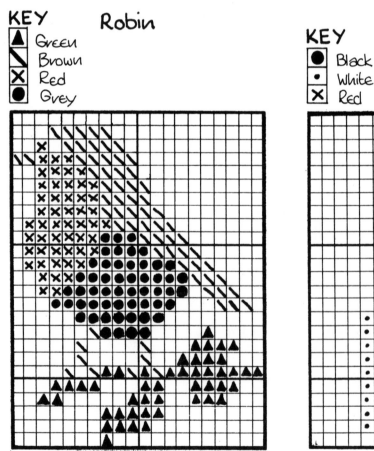

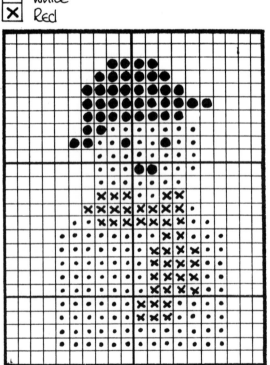

Toddler's Hooded Top

S. A. Burton, Trowbridge, Wiltshire

Make this attractive top in a warm brushed fabric for a cosy and useful present. It is made from simple rectangles only, and will fit 18 months to 3 years.

Materials

60cm brushed acrylic fabric (135cm wide)
matching thread
embroidered motif

Method

1 Cut fabric pieces as shown in Fig 1. 1cm seams are allowed throughout.
2 Fold hood in half lengthwise, right sides together and stitch back seam. Press seam open. Fold hood into triangle with seam in centre (see Fig 2) and stitch across top 5cm from point to shape hood. Trim off excess and neaten edges. Turn face edge under 1cm and topstitch.

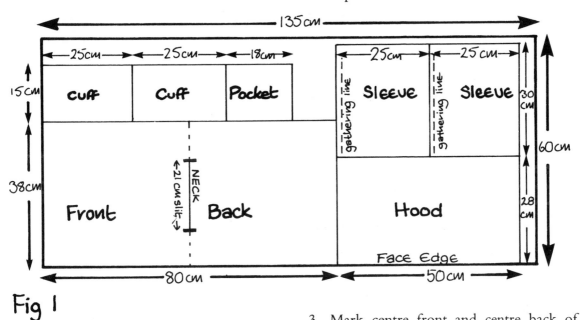

Fig 1

Fig 2

3 Mark centre front and centre back of neck opening. Pin back seam of hood to centre back of neck, and face edges to centre front, right sides together. Ease hood to fit neckline, tack and stitch.
4 Attach sleeves to body, right sides together, matching centre of sleeve to fold line on shoulder. Stitch together front and back at sides, leaving 10cm opening at bottom.
5 Stitch cuffs to sleeves, right sides together, gathering sleeves slightly to fit. Trim seam, fold cuff over, turn under 1cm and hem to line of machine stitching.
6 Turn under and topstitch side openings. Turn 2cm hem on bottom and topstitch.
7 Press under 1cm all round pocket and topstitch. Slipstitch motif to centre of pocket. Slipstitch pocket to centre of front, about 4cm from lower edge.

Embroidered Greetings Cards
Maria Weiss, St Legier, Switzerland

Embroidery in metallic thread or coloured silks is most effective on black card. It can be used on cards for all occasions, or calendars, bookmarks etc.

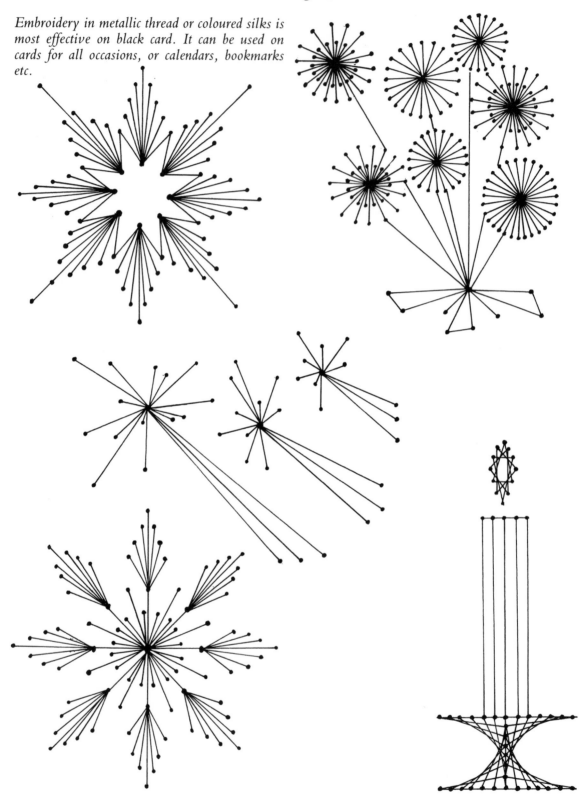

Materials

tracing paper

8cm squares of black card

scrap of polystyrene tile or flat polystyrene packing (or cork or pinboard)

metallic threads (gold and silver), or coloured embroidery threads

glue

white card folded into 11cm square greetings cards for mounting embroidery

Method

1 Place tracing paper over the required design and mark off the dots (they will be holes in card).

2 Place a square of black card on polystyrene, place design over the top and pin through two of the dots to hold in place. Pin through every dot to make holes in the card. Remove card from polystyrene.

3 Embroider through the holes, following the design. Fix ends of threads to back of card with sellotape.

4 Glue embroidery onto white card to make greetings card (giving a border of white all round).

Tapestry Panel Woven on a Bookloom

Joni Bamford, Empingham, Leicestershire

This project offers an introduction to tapestry weaving in an extremely convenient form. The bookloom is especially suitable for beginners – it is simple to set up, portable, sits comfortably on the lap or table, and reverts to being an ordinary book when the project is finished. The finished panel is approx 178×200mm, excluding fringe.

Materials

large hardback book (minimum size 254×200mm)

2 pieces of dowelling about 25mm diameter, the same length as the width of the book (broom handle pieces are ideal, or try *rigid* cardboard tubes from kitchen wrap) for tension sticks

small quantities of wool in appropriate colours, double knitting thickness or thicker (thinner wools can be used double), in different textures such as fluffy mohair, or random dyed

soft handicraft cotton or soft string for the warp (smooth to handle and strong enough to withstand tension)

large blunt wool darning needle

Method

SETTING UP THE WARP

With the spine of the book on your left, open up the front cover and lay one end of your ball of string inside. Close the book, with about 300mm of string hanging out at the bottom and the rest of the ball at the top. Place your two tension sticks horizontally across the *middle* of the book, and hold them with one hand while you wrap the string round the whole book, from the top, down the back and up around the front (see Fig 1). Start about 6–19mm in from the left hand side, and continue wrapping around both book and sticks until your have a warp width of 178mm, spacing your warp threads at around 6 per 25mm, so that you have 45 in all (the two edge threads at each side are moved together and count as one, to give 43 warps). Don't wind too tightly – just enough to hold the sticks in place – as you can adjust the tension later, but do try to keep the warp threads parallel and check they aren't crossing over each other at the back or ends of the book. When you have 45 warp threads at the front of the book, take your string once more down the back, round the bottom, and up *inside* the front cover, coming out at the top (you may need to take out one or both of your sticks to release the tension sufficiently). Cut the string, leaving about 300mm hanging from the top of the book. You don't need to fasten or tie the two ends of the warp string as they are held firmly in place by the tension of the warp itself.

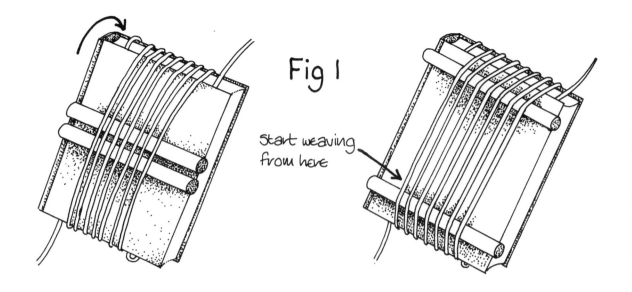

Fig 1

start weaving from here

Fig 2

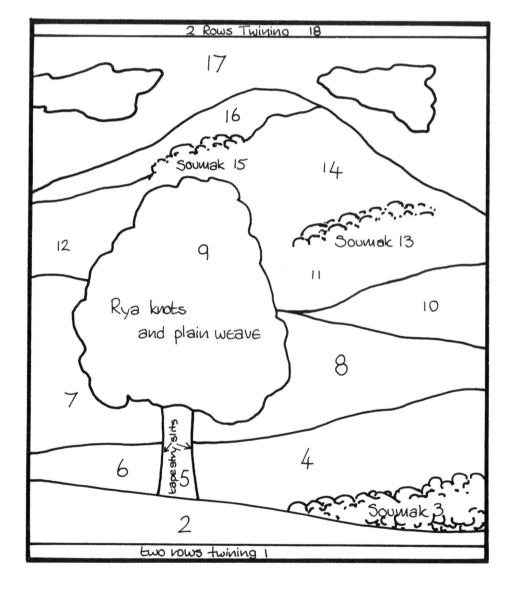

2 Rows Twining   18

17

16

Soumak 15

14

Soumak 13

12

9

11

Rya knots
and plain weave

10

7

8

tapestry slits

6

5

4

2

Soumak 3

two rows twining 1

ADJUSTING THE TENSION

Move your sticks about 180–200mm apart, so the warp becomes tighter. Check the tension by bouncing your hand across the warp threads. You may find that some parts of the warp are slacker than others, particularly at the left hand edge where you started winding. If so, to tighten up these threads start at the middle, and moving out to the left hand side, pull each warp *down* towards you in turn, taking up the slack, until you can pull the end thread tight. Now check the tension again. If you need to tighten up the right hand threads, again start from the middle and move to the right, pulling each thread this time *upwards* away from you. When weaving, tension is adjusted by moving the two sticks apart. The warp should be taut, but not so tight that you can't lift individual warp threads easily.

WEAVING THE PANEL

Make a tracing of the panel pattern (Fig 2), full size, then slide this pattern tracing on top of the book, underneath the tension sticks. You should be able to see the lines of the pattern clearly between the warp threads. Use the pattern as a guide only, making your own interpretation of the picture by using different textures and shades of colour. The numbers are a guide to the order of weaving the shapes.

Check that all your warp threads are lying parallel and evenly spaced across the book. Move the two edge threads together at each side. These will act as one warp throughout the weaving and will give a firmer edge than a single warp.

TWINING

This technique spaces the warp threads evenly and provides a firm and decorative edge for the weaving. Cut a length of warping string at least 4 times the width of the weaving, fold it in half, and loop it around the doubled left hand warp threads, just *above* the bottom stick. Take the left hand half (weft), over the edge warp and under the second warp. Adjust it so that it sits firmly against the edge warp without pulling it out of line, and leave the weft lying across the warp threads. Now take the other half of the weft (which has already gone behind the edge warp threads) over the second warp and under the third, again leaving it lying across the warp threads. Now take the first weft over the third warp, and under the fourth, making sure that it has also crossed over the other half of the weft (see Fig 3). Continue in this way across the warp, taking each half of the weft in turn, making sure that each warp thread is enclosed by the two weft threads which cross over each other in between each warp.

When you reach the right hand edge, take the left hand weft around the edge warp from front to back and out between the first and second warps, and the other weft round the edge warp from back to front, then under the second warp thread. Now work back along the warp from right to left, this time taking the right hand weft first, over one warp and under one warp, as before. Push this second row down to sit on top of the first row – it should look like a row of chain stitches. Leave the rest of the twining weft at the side; the ends can be darned in later or knotted together and included in the fringe.

PLAIN WEAVE

Plain, or tabby, weave is the basic tapestry weave, and is just like darning – the weft thread goes over one warp thread and under the next on one row, and under one warp and over the next on the second row.

You can either use a large blunt darning needle, or as in traditional tapestry work, a finger hank or butterfly, and your fingers. Try both methods to find which suits you best. To wind a butterfly, take about 2m of your green wool and twist it around your fingers, as shown in Fig 4. Pull out about 150mm to start, pulling out more as it's needed. The butterfly is a convenient way to take a length of thread through the warp without getting it tangled.

Start as shown in Fig 5. Do the first row, then weave in the loose end over just a few warp threads. (This makes a double thickness of weft when the second row is woven, but this won't show when the weft is beaten down.) It is most important when weaving *not* to pull the weft straight across the warp, but to leave it lying *in an arc* in between the warp threads, before pressing it straight

Fig 3 Twining

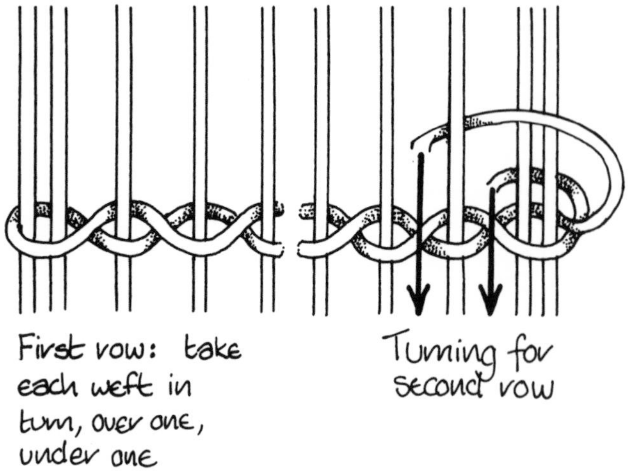

First row: take each weft in turn, over one, under one

Turning for second row

Fig 4

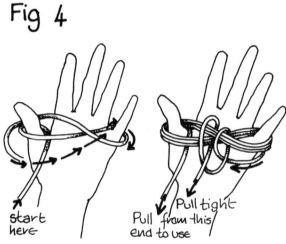

start here

Pull tight from this end to use

Fig 5 Plain Weave

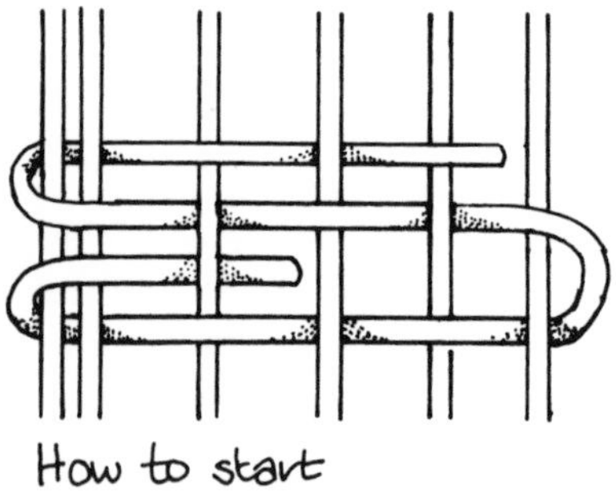

How to start

Fig 6

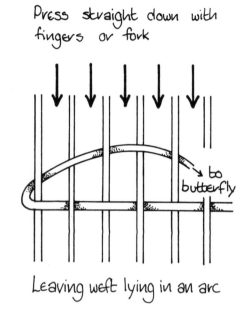

Press straight down with fingers or fork

to butterfly

Leaving weft lying in an arc

Fig 7 Shaping in plain weave

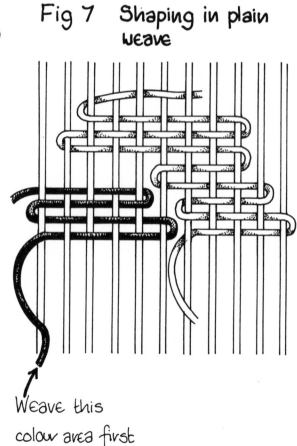

Weave this colour area first

down with the finger tips or end of the needle (see Fig 6). The strength of the finished weaving depends upon how firmly each row of weft is beaten down, and not on how tightly the weft is pulled across. The weft should cover the warp completely, bending in and out of the warp without disturbing the warp threads in any way (think of the warps as being rigid like cane so that they can't bend). After a few rows use your kitchen fork, held near the end, to beat lightly across the warp threads.

Using a butterfly and fingers is really quite simple if you follow this method. When working from left to right, hold the butterfly in your left hand, pick up three or four alternate warps in your right hand, making a space or shed between the warps, and pass the butterfly through from left to right, leaving an arc of weft. Press the weft down, then pick up the next few threads. When working from right to left, hold the butterfly in your right hand and pick up the warps with your left. Weaving is excellent exercise for the fingers – you will soon become equally happy weaving in either direction.

WEAVING SHAPES

After a few rows of plain weave in green you need to start shaping to make a curving line. Instead of going right across the warps, turn back about halfway along, just as though you'd completed a row. On the next row, turn back one or two warps earlier, following the line of your pattern, weaving just on these left hand warp threads, until you have filled in all that shape. Take care when turning – leave just enough weft to sit comfortably round the end warp without pulling the warp out of line, just as you would do at the edge.

Finish your green wool in the middle of the work, just where your next shape starts, and leave about 25mm of weft at the back of the weaving. Now continue with your next colour, bringing it out between the next two warps, again leaving about 25mm hanging at the back (these ends will be held securely when the weft is beaten down and do not need to be darned in). Weave backwards and forwards to fill in the next shape.

The numbers on the pattern indicate the best order in which to do the shapes, but you don't necessarily have to complete each shape before moving on to the next, unless the shape sits on top of another at some stage, when you *must* complete the bottom shape first (see Fig 7).

You will find when weaving the tree that there is a slit on both sides of the trunk, as you are weaving a shape with vertical sides. This is perfectly acceptable – the vertical slit is a feature of tapestry weaving – and can either be left as it is or sewn up carefully from the back afterwads. Another way would be to weave the trunk over 4 or 5 warp threads, up to where the foliage starts, then weave the background right across, taking the weft behind the trunk each time. This method has the advantage of making the trunk stand out in relief.

When weaving the rest of the tree, build up the foliage and the area on each side gradually, a few rows of each in turn, and every few rows take each weft around a common warp, to tie the different areas together. You will need two butterflies of the background weft, one for each side of the tree.

TEXTURE

Some areas of the picture are woven using other stitches for added texture, namely the tree in rya knots, and hedges in soumak. Do these as shown in Figs 8 and 9. With the rya knots, always do one row of knots followed by two rows of plain weave. Pull the loops fairly tightly on the rya knots, and either leave them as loops, or cut to form a shaggier pile. Clouds can be woven using cotton wool or a fluffy textured yarn in plain weave. Try weaving two thinner strands of wool together for a mottled effect in plain weave.

KEEPING THE EDGES STRAIGHT

It is very important to measure the weaving every few rows to make sure it is not drawing in at the edges. If you find it is starting to do this, it means you are not leaving a big enough arc of weft before beating down. Try spreading your warp threads a little wider apart at the top of the book; pull them apart at the end of each row to slacken the weft tension, and leave a

Fig 8 Rya Knots

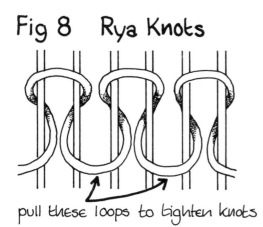

pull these loops to tighten knots

Fig 9 Soumak

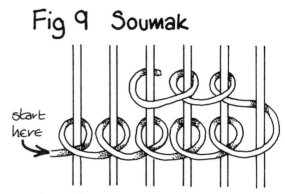

start here →

Over 2 warps, back over 1 warp
Do not pull too tight, this is a
raised stitch

longer arc – this is particularly important when using thinner wool. Make sure your warp threads are taut; the tension sticks tend to draw together as you weave, so need to be adjusted from time to time. If you find that the line of the weft tends to dip down at the edges, tighten up your edge warps, and give your weft an extra turn around the edge warps every few rows.

MOVING THE WEAVING ROUND
After weaving several centimetres you will find it harder to lift the warp threads, and need to move the weaving round the book so that more of the unwoven warp is exposed. To do this, take out the tension sticks and the patterns, slacken off the two edge warps, and carefully move the woven part of the tapestry down until the top of the weaving is about 80mm above the bottom of the book. Don't rush this – ease the weaving gently, trying to keep the bottom edge straight and the sides parallel to the sides of the book. When it is in position, fold the pattern to the right place, and put it back under the warp with the tension sticks. Tighten the warp strings and space out the warp threads before starting to weave again.

FINISHING OFF
When you reach the top of your pattern, make sure you have a level line by weaving backwards and forwards over any dips to even them up. Then do 2 rows of twining as you did at the start – this helps to secure the warp threads. Cut the warps straight across at the back of the book, leaving equal amounts of unwoven warp on each side. Taking 3 warp ends at a time (count the two

edge warps as one) plait them tightly to a suitable length, finishing with an overhand knot. Do the same both ends. If the panel is to be hung on the wall, attach a stick or piece of dowelling to the top by knotting pairs of plaits together around the stick, with the ends hanging down the back out of sight. Alternatively, instead of plaiting the warp ends at the top, attach each one to a needle and thread down alongside the next warp, and out at the back after 25mm. Tidy up the loose ends of weft at the back, by cutting them to 25mm long. Any weft ends which stick out at the top or bottom or sides should be darned inwards.

SUGGESTIONS FOR OTHER PROJECTS
Table mats Set of 4 using the same colours in each but varying the pattern. Make sure all materials are washable. Line with cotton.
Purses Make in one piece, fold over into 3 and sew up the edges. Add a lining.
Bags Small bags for a child can be made in two pieces, front and back; use iron-on interfacing on the back of each piece and line the completed bag. Weave a handle using the whole length of the warp. Larger bags can be made in units and put together patchwork-fashion. Or weave a small panel and sew it to an existing shoulder bag.
Belts Weave in 2 pieces and sew together firmly in the middle; either darn in all weft ends or add a backing.
Bookmarks The ideal present to weave on a bookloom! Use finer wool, crochet cottons or embroidery silks.

Reversible Play Cloak
M. B. Hopkins, Sketty, Swansea, West Glamorgan

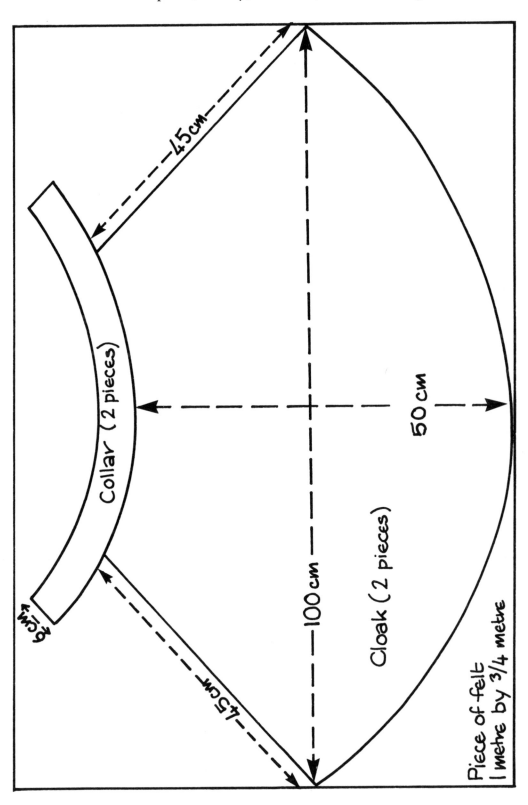

This reversible play cloak is a guaranteed hit with any 3–7 year old. One side is scarlet with a yellow crown and hearts (for King/Queen of Hearts); the other is blue with a red cross (for nurse or knight). Endless fun is assured and there are so many variations – Superman/Spiderman, Robin Hood/Sheriff of Nottingham etc, etc. For a different look, you could make tabards instead.

Materials

1×75m red felt

1×75m blue mid-weight cotton (an old gored skirt is ideal)

scrap of red cotton fabric for one side of collar

scraps of felt; red for cross, yellow for crown and 4 hearts

matching threads

blue or red button

Method

1 Following diagram, cut a cloak and collar piece from red felt, a cloak piece from blue cotton and a collar piece from red cotton. (Using the two materials makes the cloak hang properly and enables you to use up old fabrics. An all-felt cloak would be too stiff.)

2 Using templates, cut red felt cross (in strips if necessary), yellow felt crown and 4

hearts. Position cross on felt cloak piece, crown etc on blue cloak piece, in the centre. (Place hearts round crown.) Stitch each motif in place, round the edge, by hand or machine. Use matching threads and small neat stitches.

3 Place cloak pieces right sides together and sew round bottom and sides, 1cm from edge (leave top open). Mitre curved edges if necessary. Turn through and topstitch over seams, using red thread. This gives a firm, strong edge.

4 Place collar pieces right sides together and stitch round top and sides (1cm from edge), leaving bottom open to join to cloak. Turn through and topstitch over seams. Turn open edges under and fit carefully over top of cloak. Tack. Stitch through all layers.

5 Make buttonhole in one end of collar and stitch button to other end.

Nursery Picture – Goosey Goosey Gander

Julia D. Simkin, Erdington, Birmingham

A bright nursery picture is the ideal gift for a baby – and it is simple to design your own from a children's picture book. A second idea is given for Mary Had a Little Lamb or Baa Baa Black Sheep, which could start you off on a whole series of pictures.

Materials

16×20cm canvas

scraps of tapestry wool or embroidery thread (not both) in white, dark green, light green, dark brown, mid brown, grey/blue, orange and dark grey/black

Method

1 Draw out the design on graph paper, then transfer to canvas, 1 square on the paper to 1 hole on the canvas.

2 Work the picture in half cross stich or tramming, following the colour guide.

3 When completed, block out, steam and stretch. Then have the picture framed.

KEY

- • grey/blue
- ▲ dark green
- △ light green
- ☐ white
- ✕ orange
- ● mid brown
- ◥ dark brown

KEY

·	grey/blue
▲	dark green
△	light green
○	gold
☐	white or black
●	mid brown

Suggested 'Mary Had a Little Lamb' or colour the sheep black for 'Baa Baa Black Sheep'

Strawberry Workbox

Margaret K. Blakeley, Heywood, Lancashire

This original little workbox (203×100×63mm) is cleverly designed and simply made from fabric-covered pieces of card, glued and sewn together. It even has a 'hinged' lid. Inside are a matching neddlecase, strawberry pincushion, and elasticated pockets and straps to hold scissors, tape measure, large needles etc. The perfect gift for a needle-woman, or perhaps a child's first workbox.

Materials

sheet or pieces of 3mm thick card (not corrugated)
40×40cm felt (any colour)
Copydex glue
0.5m light-green cotton fabric
sheet or pieces of thin card
50×50cm wadding
0.5m floral cotton fabric for lining
scraps of elastic
UHU glue
scraps of iron-on Vilene
scraps of leaf-green cotton fabric
scraps of red cotton fabric
yellow and green embroidery threads
tiny scraps of cream fabric
scraps of stuffing
scrap of green flannel or coarse woven fabric for inside of needlecase
scrap of thin ribbon
matching threads

Method

1 Following measurements in Fig 1, cut base, ends and sides from 3mm card, to give 5 separate pieces. Cut same pieces in felt and stick felt to outside of box, using Copydex. (Use Copydex throughout, unless directed otherwise.) Always check measurements, as slight difference in thickness of card may necessitate adjustments.
2 Cut base, ends and sides in light-green fabric, allowing extra 10mm all round for turnings. Use to cover outside of box pieces, sticking turnings only, on inside.
3 Slipstitch ends to base firmly from outside, holding them at right-angles as you stitch. Similarly stitch sides to base, then slipstitch up corners.

4 Using thin card, cut pieces to line inside of box, finishing 6mm below top edge of box all round. Cover inside of these pieces as before but with wadding and then floral lining fabric. Before covering the sides, make gathered pockets from floral fabric with elastic in a casing at the top, to fit along length of sides. Stitch to fabric lining before sticking. Stitch covered pieces together at corners, then stick into green box using UHU.

LID

1 Following measurements in Fig 1, cut lid pieces from 3mm card. Cut same pieces in wadding and stick to outside of lid. Cut 2 pieces light-green fabric, each 215×120mm. Place wrong sides together, stitch round edges, leaving one end open, trim corners and turn through.
2 Push one of larger pieces of card inside fabric to end and machine across to hold in place. Push in small piece and repeat stitching. Push in third piece of card, turn under ends of fabric and slipstitch closed.
3 Cut 2 pieces thin card 90×76mm. Cut 2 pieces lining fabric 114×100mm. Make 2 covered elastic straps (using lining fabric) and place across centre of shorter sides of fabric pieces, stitching at the edges. One of these straps will hold the needlecase. The other can be stitched down at intervals to make slots for bodkins, darning needles etc.
4 Cover thin-card pieces with fabric pieces, sticking down turnings or ladder-stitching across both ways for firmness. Place lining cards to underside of lid, about 6mm from outside edges all round so that lid will close right down.

LEAVES

1 Iron Vilene onto half of leaf-green fabric, on wrong side. Place the two halves wrong sides together, tack. Using patterns given in Fig 2, trace 2 of each of leaves onto fabric. Machine round outline and cut out just outside stitching. Satin stitch round edges. Add veining in straight stitch.
2 Stitch leaves to box lid, stitching under

Fig 1   Box

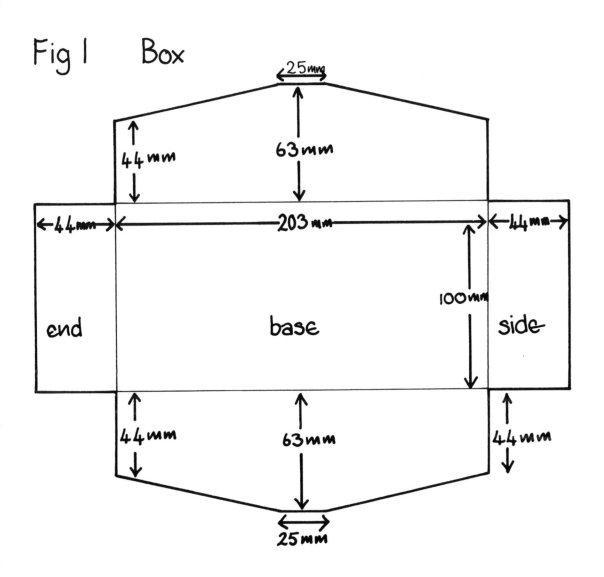

25mm		

44 mm

63mm

44mm | 203 mm | 44mm

end | base | side

100mm

44mm | 63mm | 44mm

25mm

Lid

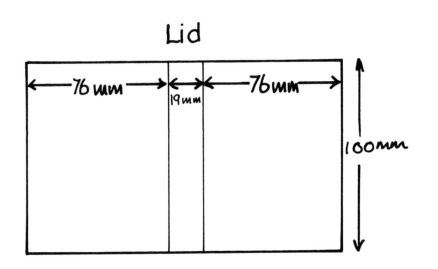

76 mm | 19mm | 76mm

100mm

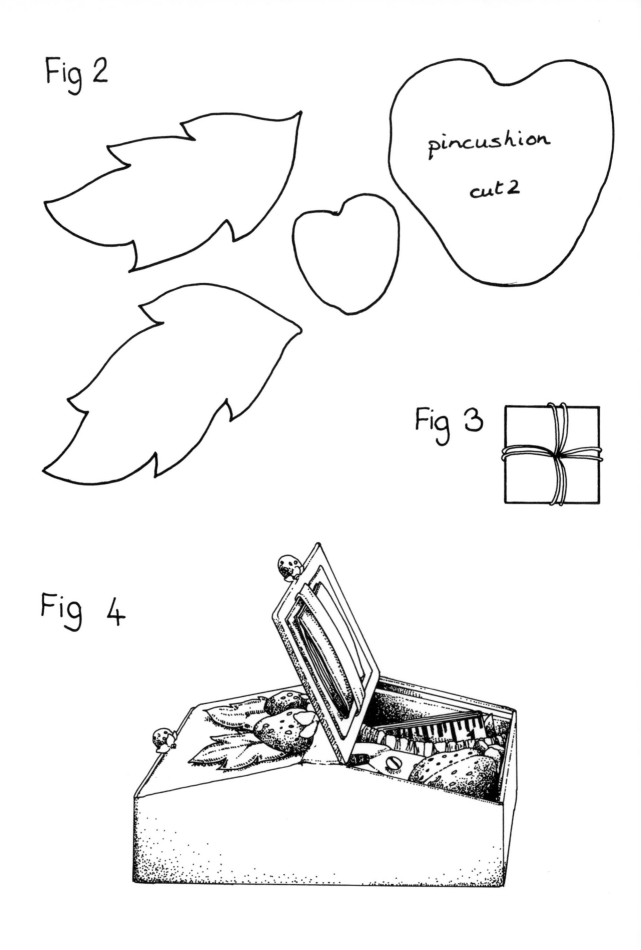

Fig 2

pincushion

cut 2

Fig 3

Fig 4

leaves so it does not show (wadding on lid helps here).

STRAWBERRIES

1 Cut 2 pattern pieces (using Fig 2) for each strawberry, one with extra 6mm all round for turnings (there are 4 strawberries on lid).
2 Gather edge of larger piece to fit smaller. Place wrong sides together and backstitch round edge, leaving opening at top. Turn through, stuff firmly and slipstitch closed. Stitch seeds with yellow embroidery thread.
3 To make husk, cut 25×50mm piece of leaf-green fabric. Fold wrong sides together to make a square and backstitch round three sides. Turn through and slipstitch remaining side. With double green thread, make a backstitch in centre of square, then 2 stitches with the thread going round each side (see Fig 3). Pull stitches tight to make husk shape. Stitch husk to top of strawberry. Stitch strawberry in position on lid.

FLOWERS

1 Cut 4 circles of cream fabric, 20mm diameter. For each flower, gather round edge, pull up tightly and fasten off.
2 With green thread, stitch from centre round edge as with husks, pulling slightly to make petal shape. Embroider yellow stamens in centres. Stitch onto lid.

KNOBS

1 Make 2 tiny strawberries for knobs from 20mm diameter circles of light-green fabric. Gather round, stuff firmly and pull up tightly. Embroider green seeds. Make tiny husks from 25×12.5mm pieces of leaf-green fabric as described above. Sew husk over gathering and sew firmly to edge of lid.
2 Sew lid neatly to box in 4 places where machine stitching forms 'hinge'.

NEEDLECASE

1 Cut 2 pieces of fabric 90×130mm, one light green, one of lining fabric. Wrong sides together, stitch round 3 sides, turn through, turn in remaining edges. Cut pieces of felt slightly smaller and place inside, lying flat. Topstitch all round 3mm from edge.
2 Cut piece of flannel slightly smaller than case and stitch in place through 'spine' of case. Finish with a ribbon bow through 'spine'.

STRAWBERRY PINCUSHION

1 Cut 2 pattern pieces from red fabric (Fig 2). Wrong sides together, stitch round edge leaving opening at top. Turn through, stuff tightly, slipstitch top. Stitch seeds with embroidery thread.
2 Make husk from 35×70mm piece of leaf-green fabric, and stitch in place.

Decorative Handbag

Margaret Shaw, Clitheroe, Lancashire

With this basic pattern you can make a handbag to match or tone with any outfit. The pattern provides for a short handle but to make a shoulder bag make the handle section 92cm long. The bag can be decorated with braid, ribbon, beads or whatever takes your fancy.

Materials

2 pieces of fabric, one 20×36cm for bag and one 3×45cm for handle
2 pieces of heavy-duty iron-on interlining or plastic 'canvas' the same sizes

2 pieces of lining same size as above.

Method

1 Iron on the interlining (if used) to the outer fabric and tack to the lining of both the main piece and the handle. Alternatively, tack lining and main fabric to plastic canvas.
2 Assemble the bag by folding along the lines indicated in the diagram and insert the strip to form side gussets and handle.
3 Oversew into position.
4 Sew on decoration.

Party Bag

Ann Mary Johnstone, Haddenham, Aylesbury, Buckinghamshire

A party bag decorated with ribbons and machine embroidery, and made simply from two flat pieces joined together with a gusset. It could be made to match a special outfit, or hand embroidered instead of machine stitched.

Materials

25×48cm plain-coloured fabric
25×48cm contrasting coloured fabric for lining
23×48cm pelmet-weight Vilene
50cm toning velvet ribbon or petersham for gusset (longer if handle or shoulder strap required)
toning ribbons and thread for decoration
glue
8cm diameter circle lightweight fabric for rosette
small button for rosette
press stud

Method

1 Make pattern for front: draw semi-circle 20cm across. Add a 3cm strip to straight edge (Fig 1).
2 Make pattern for back and flap (one piece): draw as for front; add further strip of 2cm to straight edge; then add another semi-circle the same size as before to form flap (Fig 2).
3 Using these patterns, cut a front and back from main fabric, adding 2cm extra all round for turnings. Repeat, cutting from lining fabric. Then cut front and back from Vilene, without adding extra for turnings.
4 Do any hand embroidering next.

5 Tack Vilene pieces to pieces of main fabric. Tack guide lines for machine embroidery. These must be absolutely straight, and lines on flap must match lines on front exactly (if using vertical lines as in bag shown). The decoration should continue from front right round to back. Work decoration, sewing through both layers, stitching down ribbons with zig-zag and other machine embroidery (Fig 3).
6 Snip turnings at 1cm intervals and stick down onto Vilene, mitreing the corners of the front (Fig 4).
7 To make rosette, make a tiny hem round the circle of fabric using running stitches and strong thread. Draw stitches up tight to gather, and fasten off securely. Gather a small piece of ribbon to make the middle of the rosette, and place the button at the centre. Stitch to front of flap, over position of press stud.
8 Snip the turnings of lining pieces and turn in. Slipstitch linings to front and back pieces.
9 Front and back are joined with a gusset (Fig 5). Make a tiny hem in one end of velvet ribbon and ladderstitch neatly to inside edge of front. Hem other end of ribbon. (This method is safer than trying to cut an exact length first.) If strap is wanted, omit second hem and continue ribbon to required length, attaching the end to first hem. Pin back to gusset, matching lines of decoration, and ladderstitch.
10 Attach press stud under rosette, aligning pattern on front and flap.

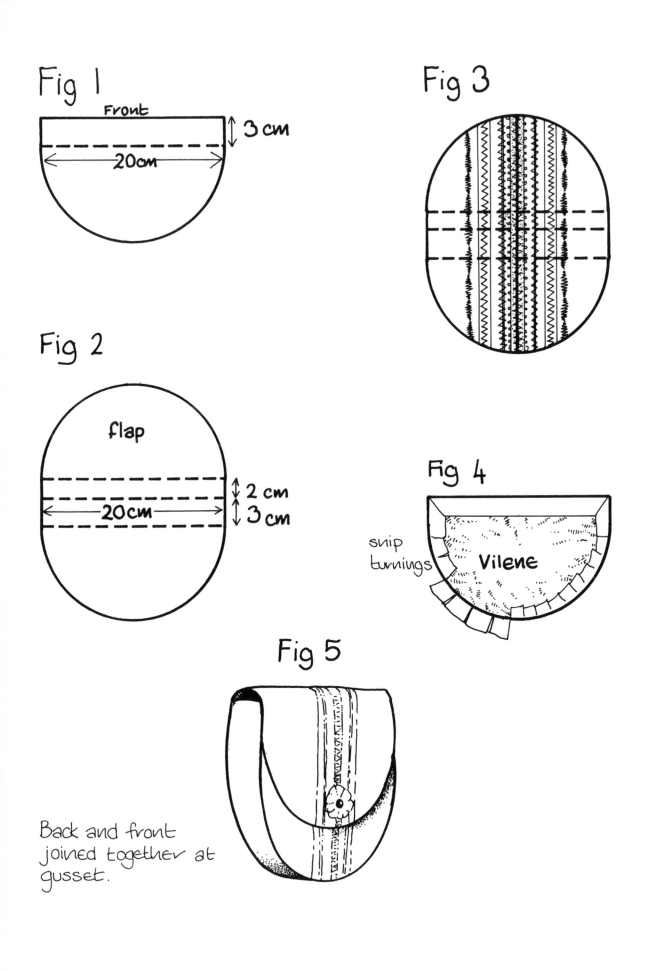

Fig 1

Front

3 cm

20cm

Fig 2

flap

2 cm
3 cm

20cm

Fig 3

Fig 4

snip
turnings

Vilene

Fig 5

Back and front
joined together at
gusset.

BAZAAR BESTSELLERS *(opposite)*
1 Christmas decorations *(page 141)*
2 Padded hanger with potpourri heart *(page 133)*
3 Appliquéd fabric box *(page 134)*
4 Cheshire and Isle of Wight cottage pincushions *(page 126)*
5 Smocked lavender sachet *(page 128)*
6 Suffolk puff clowns *(page 136)*
7 Heart-shaped brooches *(page 140)*
8 Strawberry emery *(page 138)*

SEWING AND EMBROIDERY *(overleaf)*
1 Reversible play cloak – also shown on page 84 *(page 105)*
2 Decorative handbag *(page 113)*
3 Strawberry workbox *(page 110)*
4 Party bag *(page 114)*
5 Embroidered greetings cards *(page 98)*
6 Applied embroidered fabric picture *(page 122)*
7 Full-fringed tablecloth and napkins *(page 124)*

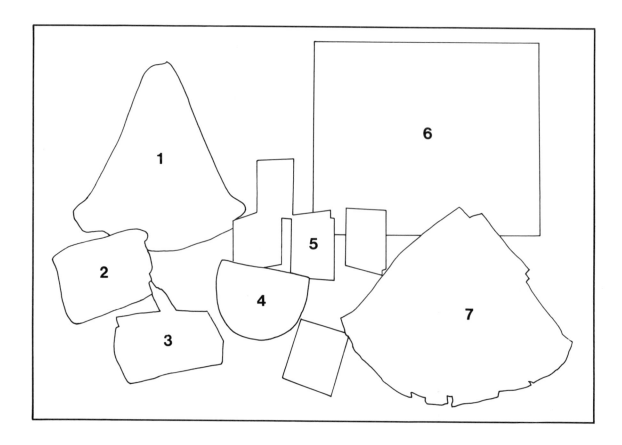

BAZAAR BESTSELLERS *(opposite)*

1 Knitting bag and needle roll *(page 143)*
2 Play-and-learn collage *(page 130)*
3 Peg bag *(page 139)*
4 Hand-printed scarf *(page 144)*
5 Play apron *(page 142)*

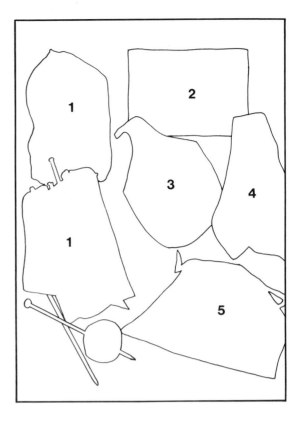

Applied Embroidered Fabric Picture

Phyllis Watts, Bayston Hill, Shrewsbury. Shropshire

The basis of this unique picture is a large, simple flower pattern in a curtain fabric. The flower has been outlined and decorated with embroidery, then cut out of the fabric, rearranged and glued onto a contrasting backing material. Original and effective, it is a clever way of developing your own embroidery and design skills, without starting completely from scratch. (It also gives you a picture to tone in with your curtains.) The picture shown measures 50×60cm (framed), but size will depend on your chosen pattern.

Materials

remnant of soft, closely woven curtain material (lightweight) with clear, large flower pattern

stranded embroidery threads to match colours in fabric

gold or antique-gold metallic thread for highlighting

sequins and beads to decorate flower centres

backing material in suitable contrasting colour

thick card or hardboard for mounting picture

strong thread for mounting

all-purpose clear adhesive

frame and glass if required

Method

1   Choose the flowers you want to use and work a row of chain stitch (2 strands) round edges of outer petals (for padding). If edges are fussy, keep basic shape, but simplify. Work over chain stitch with closely packed buttonhole stitch, using thread to match colour of petals (2 strands).

2   Embroider round edges of remaining petals with double-knot stitch (3 strands).

3   Where you can see the flower centre, work a ring of rosette chain stitch in metallic thread (6 strands). Fill in centres with sequins, each one sewn down with a small bead.

4   If there are shading lines on the petals, highlight some with random Cretan stitch in metallic thread (1 strand).

5   Outline chosen leaves as for flowers.

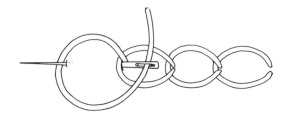

Fig 1 Chain Stitch

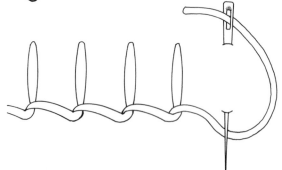

Fig 2 Buttonhole Stitch

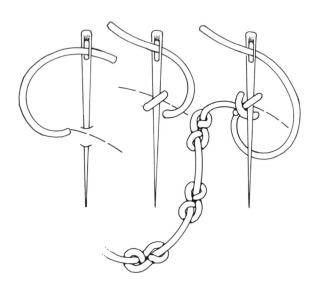

Fig 3 Double Knot Stitch

Fig 4 Rosette Chain Stitch

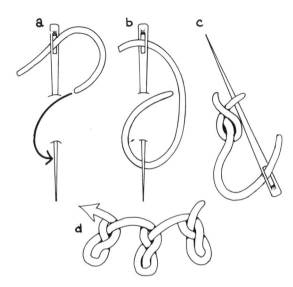

a b c

d

Fig 5 Random Cretan Stitch

a

b

c

(variations)

Fig 6 Couching

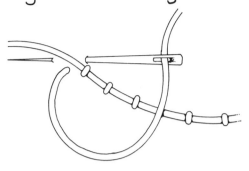

Fig 7 Stem Stitch

Fig 8   Long and Short Stitch

a

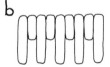

b

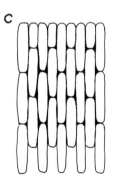

c

Work centre veins in metallic thread using chain stitch (2 strands), couched-down thread or perhaps Spanish knotted stitch. Work side veins in stem stitch or long stitch in metallic thread (1 strand). Choose the stitch which suits the size of leaves.

6   Work down one side of each stem in buttonhole stitch, then up the other side, stitching in between first stitches. If there are no suitable stems on the fabric, work your own on a plain piece of the fabric. (The water lilies in the picture illustrated do not need stems as they are meant to be on top of the water.)

7   When you have completed enough flowers, leaves and stems, use sharp embroidery scissors to cut them out, carefully, so that there is no fabric surrounding them. Press lightly on the wrong side on top of a folded towel, with a warm iron.

8   Mount backing materials onto card or hardboard by lacing with strong thread at the back.

9   Arrange the embroidered pieces into a pleasing design on the backing. As in flower arranging, smaller pieces should be at the top. Stems should carry down through the design and show at the bottom. Take time to get the design right, then glue each piece down, using adhesive sparingly and spreading it with a matchstick. Overlap some of petals and leaves as in real life. Pat down with a soft cloth to remove all air from underside. Leave 24 hours to dry.

10   Place in a frame behind glass for best results.

11   Once you are adept at flowers, you may like to experiment with different embroidery stitches and incorporate animal or butterfly motifs (see colour picture).

Full-fringed Tablecloth and Napkins

Julia Simkin, Erdington, Birmingham

A matching tablecloth and napkin set can be a most useful present if care is taken to match the room it is intended for. This set is in a pretty lilac linen fabric with contrasting mauve embroidery and luxurious full fringe. Use hand or machine embroidery, or a mixture of the two. The tablecloth is 150cm square, and there are 6 napkins.

Materials

2.5m moygashel, woven linen fabric (150cm wide)
contrasting thread (or embroidery silk)

Method

1   Cut a 150cm square and trim off selvedges. Strip threads from edges to level sides, and trim frayed edges.

2   Measure 2.5–5cm from edges (depending on width of fringe required), and mark a cross at this point in each corner. Strip threads from each edge until crosses have disappeared, to make fringe.

3   Using zig-zag stitch, embroider a pattern just inside the fringed edges to prevent further fraying. Add a second line of embroidery inside the first to complete tablecloth, using a stitch or motif of your choice.

4   Cut remaining fabric into 6 pieces and treat as tablecloth. These look best with only the first line of embroidery.

5   Press well with a damp cloth.

Bazaar Bestsellers

colour photographs on pages 117 and 120

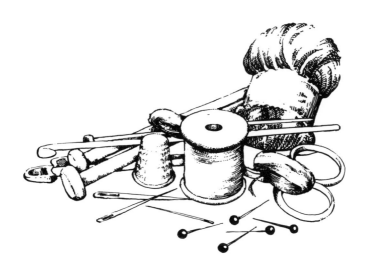

Cheshire and Isle of Wight cottage pincushions   126

Smocked lavender sachet   128

Play-and-learn collage   130

Padded hanger with potpourri heart   133

Appliquéd fabric box   134

Suffolk puff clown   136

Strawberry emery   138

Peg bag   139

Heart-shaped brooches   140

Christmas decorations   141

Play apron   142

Knitting bag and needle roll   143

Hand-printed scarf   144

Cheshire and Isle of Wight Cottage Pincushions

V. Goodbury, West Malvern, Hereford and Worcester

These character cottages (8×5×7cm) could start you off on a whole collection of regional styles, almost too appealing to use as pincushions. They are simply made from felt and card, with embroidered architectural details, and the idea is easily adapted to any building.

Materials

15cm square of white felt for timbered Cheshire cottage; or stone for brick-and-thatch Isle of Wight cottage

9cm square of grey felt for roof

scraps of felt for door and windows: red and grey for Cheshire; green and light blue for Isle of Wight

scraps of thin card

stranded embroidery cotton: black, white and dark brown for Cheshire; black, white, stone (or beige), 'brick' and grey for Isle of Wight

matching threads

scraps of stuffing

UHU glue

Method

Cut pattern pieces (Fig 1) from appropriate coloured felt. Cut card pieces 2mm smaller all round for base, ends and walls (not roof). Slipstitch door and windows to felt front wall, then embroider details as follows (numbers in brackets indicate strands of embroidery cotton).

ISLE OF WIGHT COTTAGE (opposite left)

1 Work window panes in white (2) backstitch, and door knocker and letter box in black (2).

2 Work window sills and lintels in stone or beige (4) bokhara couching.

3 Work brick features round windows and door in 'brick' colour (2) satin stitch.

4 Work thatch detail round lower and side edges of roof, plus a few stitches on porch in grey (2) herringbone. Stitch porch thatch in position, leaving lower edge open.

CHESHIRE COTTAGE (opposite right)

1 Embroider window panes in white (2), single stitches woven as you work to give neater finish.

2 Work door knocker and frame in dark brown (6) stem stitch.

3 Work beams in black (4) split stitch. These do not have to be exactly as shown, as no two cottages are alike.

To make up

1 Stitch felt ends to front and back walls. Stitch base in place.

2 Stick card pieces lightly inside felt pieces.

3 Embroider brick feature on front corners of Isle of Wight cottage, as before.

4 Stitch roof pieces to walls, starting at the ridge and working down. Allow to overlap walls to make eaves along lower edges – stitch underside of eaves carefully to top of walls.

5 Stuff firmly, taking care not to distort roof.

6 Sew roof ridge with buttonhole stitch.

7 Stitch chimney pieces together and sew in place.

Fig 1

Walls and Roof
Cut 2 white or stone
Cut 2 grey
Cut 2 card

Base
Cut 1 white or stone
Cut 1 card

Base End Wall
Cut 2 white or stone
Cut 2 card

Upper Window
Cut 2

Lower Window
Cut 2

Chimney
Cut 2 of each
white or stone

Porch Thatch
Cut 1 grey (row only)

Door
Cut 1

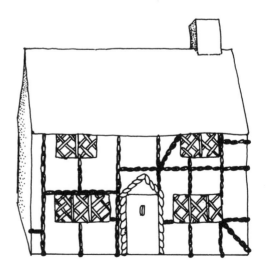

Smocked Lavender Sachet

N. Margerum, Northolt, Greater London

Everyone loves a gift of sweet-smelling herbs, and this delicate little smocked sachet (12×8cm) makes the perfect container. Filled with sawdust and sand, it could also be used as a pincushion.

Materials

smocking dot transfer, size 6×9mm (¼×⅜in)
100×510mm white cotton
strong white thread
stranded embroidery cotton in green, pink and light brown for smocking
760mm white lace (25mm wide)
150mm narrow white ribbon
100×130mm white cotton
2 pieces 130×76mm calico
small amount of lavender to fill sachet

Method

1 Transfer smocking dots to reverse of large piece of white cotton. Pick up dots with running stitches, using strong sewing thread. Start each row with a secure knot and a length of thread at least 760mm long. Do not fasten off at the end of rows (Fig 1) at this stage.

2 Pull up gathering threads so fabric forms even tubes as in Fig 2 (fabric should be about ⅓ original length). Tie ends together in pairs, securely. Hold hot steam iron over back of fabric, but do not put weight of iron on fabric.

4 Work smocking design as shown on chart in Fig 3 (each vertical line represents a tube of fabric, each horizontal line is a gathering thread). When completed, pull out gathering threads.

5 Gather lace. Place gathered edge of lace to edge of smocking on the right side, with lace pointing in towards centre of smocking. Fold ribbon in half and place in one corner, on top of lace, with fold towards centre of smocking. Tack round all four edges of smocking, through ribbon and lace (Fig 4).

6 Place smaller piece of white cotton on top of smocking, right sides together. Machine round three edges. Turn through.

7 Place calico pieces right sides together, machine round three sides, turn through. Fill with lavender, turn in open edges and oversew firmly.

8 Place lavender bag inside smocked bag, turn in edges and slipstitch neatly, stitching through lace.

Fig 1
Transfer dots and gathering

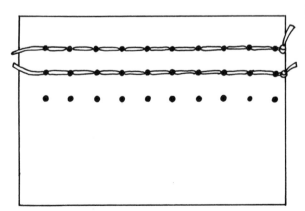

Fig 2
Pulled up gathering threads to form tubes

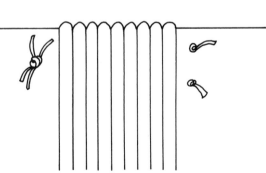

Fig 3 Smocking Design

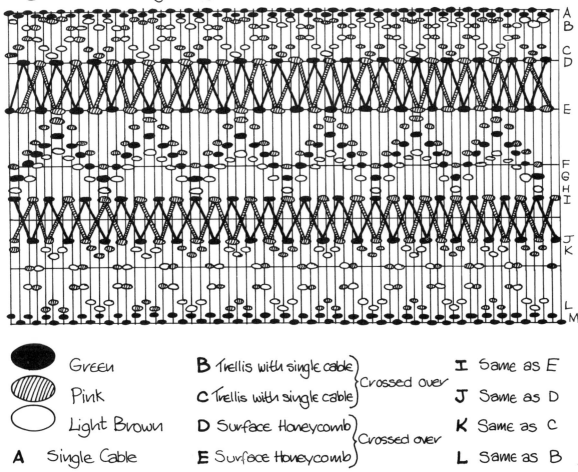

A
B
C
D
E
F
G
H
I
J
K
L
M

⬬ Green	
▨ Pink	
⬭ Light Brown	
A Single Cable	

B Trellis with single cable ⎫
C Trellis with single cable ⎬ Crossed over
D Surface Honeycomb ⎫
E Surface Honeycomb ⎬ Crossed over
F, G+H Trellis

I Same as E
J Same as D
K Same as C
L Same as B
M Same as A

Fig 4

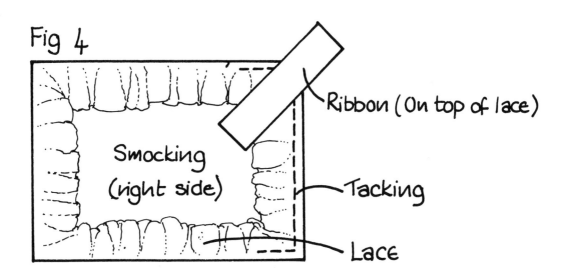

Ribbon (On top of lace)

Smocking
(right side)

Tacking

Lace

Play-and-learn Collage

C. Andrews, Southend-on-Sea, Essex

This imaginative collage incorporates a zip, buttons, laces, a hook-and-eye and press stud, which young children can fasten and unfasten – and thus learn to cope with the variety of fastenings on today's clothing. Many other fastenings could be included (eg, buckles or Velcro) with only minor adjustments to the pattern, which could even be enlarged to life size (this one is about 40×30cm).

Materials

glue and/or matching threads
scraps of fabric for collage pieces
white paper (writing thickness) for lining pieces
42×32cm backing fabric
2 pieces 40×30cm medium-strength cardboard
2 buttons
14cm zip
scraps of wool for hair
scrap of narrow ribbon for bonnet
bootlace
large hook-and-eye
large press stud

Method

1 Cut out collage pieces using patterns. If you want to sew them down (rather than sticking them) add seam allowances. Cut paper linings for all pieces except jacket and cape. Neaten edges which are not to be sewn.

2 Fold backing fabric over one piece of card and lightly mark picture area. Remove from card.

3 Stick or sew pieces to backing fabric (position them first), starting with legs and feet, then adding shirt, tie, dress and hands.

4 Make buttonholes on jacket where marked on pattern, and attach buttons on other side where marked. Place jacket in

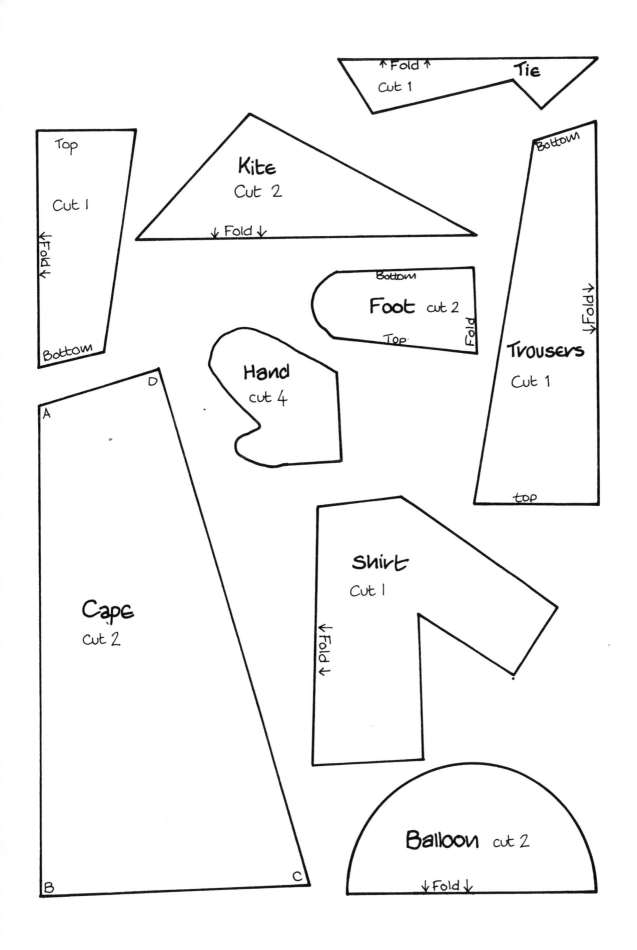

position, buttons under buttonholes, then sew or glue down the sides only, A to E to D.

5   Sew zip to sides AB of cape. Fold shoulders of cape into required shape. Position on collage then sew or glue sides A to C.

6   Make plait for girl and cut short strands for boy's hair. Stick onto back lower edges of cap and bonnet pieces (between A and B on cap). Fix ribbon to bonnet. Stick or sew bonnet and cap in position.

7   Sew or stick the two kite pieces together with paper lining in the middle. Attach a piece of bootlace to lower corner. Make up

balloon in same way. Attach kite and balloon to outside hands of children with hook-and-eye and press stud. Sew kite and balloon strings (lace) firmly to collage to prevent loss.

8   Place collage over one piece of cardboard and glue turnings down. Stick second piece of cardboard to back to strengthen.

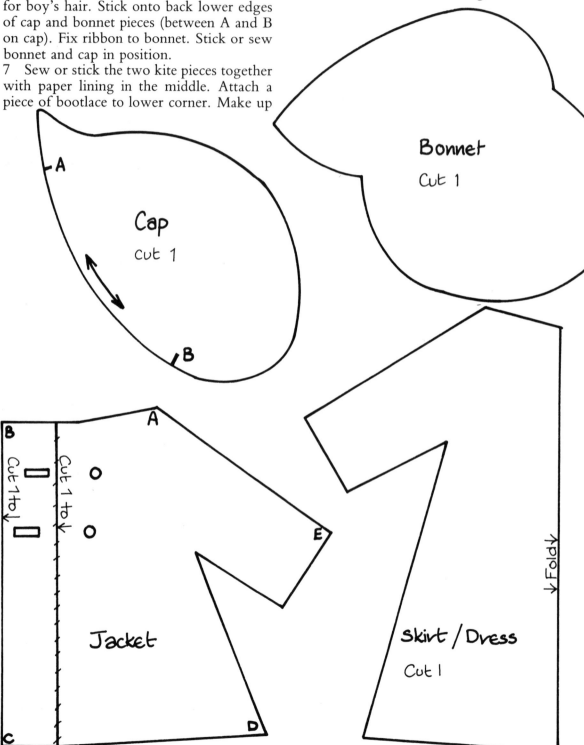

Padded Hanger with Pot-pourri Heart

S. Clarke, Beeston, Nottingham

This ever-popular idea is always a useful gift, and especially welcome with its fragrant 'heart of flowers'.

Materials

standard wooden coat hanger
200mm hollow white bootlace (or corset lacing) to cover hook
500×140mm thick terylene wadding
0.5m soft cotton fabric with pretty (small) floral print
scrap of white cotton for heart
300mm narrow white lace
800mm narrow coloured ribbon, toning with main fabric
small amount pot-pourri

Method

1 Cut a length of bootlace slightly longer than hook. Turn in edges at one end and sew neatly. Push hook into lace, pull tightly and fasten securely at base of hook.

2 Cut wadding to fit round hangar and sew in place, with seam along top and down sides.

3 Cut piece of cotton fabric to approximately twice the length by three times the width of padded hanger (not including hook). Fold in half, right sides together, and sew 12mm seams along short sides, using double thread and running stitches. Pull up slightly and fasten off. Turn through and press, also pressing long folded (bottom) edge.

4 Press 12mm turnings along open edges (ie, top). Run gathering threads along lower folded edge, from sides to middle, using double thread and stitching 6mm from fold (Fig 1), but do not pull up gathers.

5 Position cover round hanger and pin at centre. Run gathering threads along top edge, starting from sides as before, and stitching through all layers. Pull up top and bottom gathers on one side, then the other side (Fig 2). Adjust for even finish and tie off securely.

6 Cut 2 white cotton pieces using heart pattern (Fig 3). Right sides together, sew 12mm seams round edges, leaving gap between notches. Slit to dot marked on

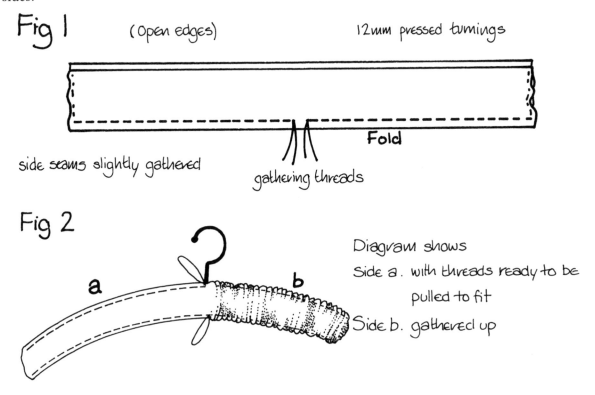

Fig I   (Open edges)   12mm pressed turnings

side seams slightly gathered   gathering threads   Fold

Fig 2

a   b

Diagram shows
Side a. with threads ready to be
pulled to fit
Side b. gathered up

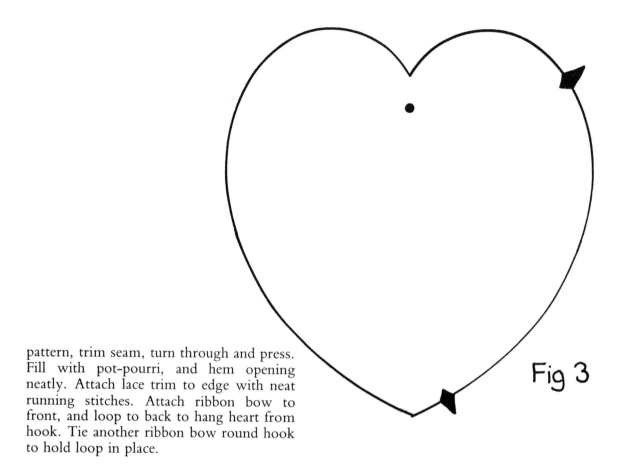

Fig 3

pattern, trim seam, turn through and press. Fill with pot-pourri, and hem opening neatly. Attach lace trim to edge with neat running stitches. Attach ribbon bow to front, and loop to back to hang heart from hook. Tie another ribbon bow round hook to hold loop in place.

Appliquéd Fabric Box
Lorna E. Liddell, Elgin, Grampian

A fabric-covered box can be just as effective as pottery or wood, and much cheaper. This one measures 9cm in diameter and would be ideal for jewellery on a dressing table.

Materials
sheet of stiff card
scrap of plain cotton fabric
scrap of toning pattern fabric (with flowers to appliqué on lid)
bead for lid handle
strong sticky tape
scrap of wadding (optional)

Method
1   Plan diameter and depth of the box. Using compasses, draw 4 circles on card, each one 3mm shorter in radius than the previous one. These are respectively: A, the lid; B, the base; C, the base liner; D, the lid liner.

2   Cut 2 strips of card E, the side and F, the side liner. E measures the circumference of B by the depth of finished box. F measures the circumference of C by the depth of the box (less 3mm on the depth). Check that each section fits together, as these measurements can only be a guide.

3   Using these pieces as patterns, cut the fabric, adding 2cm all round to each pattern: plain fabric for A, B, E; patterned for C, D, F. Cut E and F on the cross for a neat fit.

4   Appliqué flowers from patterned fabric to A, the lid, and sew bead onto centre for handle (Fig 1).

5   Run a gathering thread round each fabric

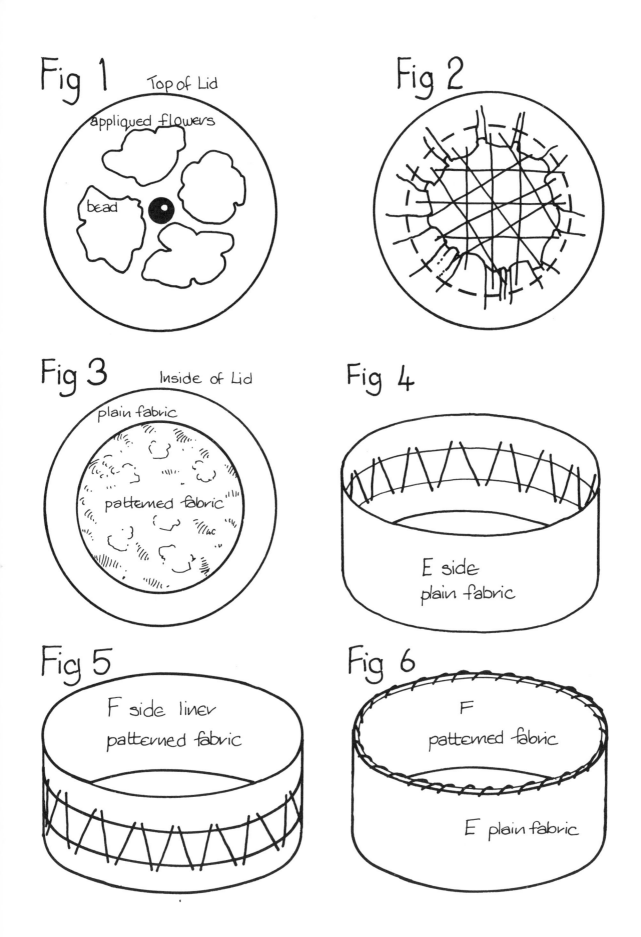

Fig 1

Top of Lid

appliqued flowers

bead

Fig 2

Fig 3

Inside of Lid

plain fabric

patterned fabric

Fig 4

E side
plain fabric

Fig 5

F side liner
patterned fabric

Fig 6

F
patterned fabric

E plain fabric

circle, insert appropriate card circle, draw up gathers, then lace fabric across tightly (Fig 2). If a softer look is required, stick wadding to card pieces A and D before covering with fabric. Sew A and D together, using a curved needle, to make lid (Fig 3).

6   Hold card pieces E and F in the steam from a kettle until they curl. Wrap round a small soup tin or similar and leave overnight to set into shape. Place card piece E (side) round circumference of B (base) and trim E if necessary. Ends should just meet; tape them together to form sides of box. Seam ends of fabric strip E together to fit card, then fit fabric over outside of card and lace on the inside (Fig 4). Oversew sides E to base B.

7   Fit side liner F inside box (Fig 5) and trim if necessary. Cover with fabric as for E, but this time fabric should cover *inside* of liner, and be laced on the outside. Oversew side liner F to base liner C.

8   Position finished lining inside box and oversew top edges together round rim of box (Fig 6).

Suffolk Puff Clown

Mary Wyatt, Crowborough, Sussex

This bright and cheerful little clown (19cm tall) makes a lovely baby's toy, and is simple and cheap to make. Use two colours throughout, alternately, or as contrast on body, collar, cuffs and pom-pom.

Materials
scraps of polyester jersey in main colour (not double kits which are too bulky)
scraps of polyester jersey in second colour for collar, cuffs and pom-pom, or as required
matching threads plus red and blue for face
50cm round cord elastic
2 large-eyed needles for threading elastic
scraps of cream or white polyester jersey for face
scrap of polyester wadding or cotton wool for stuffing
scraps of felt: flesh coloured for hands, brown for feet

Method
1   Cut all pattern pieces as indicated.
2   Make the 40 medium-sized circles into Suffolk puffs. Sew round edge of circle with small running stitches, beginning with a good knot and a backstitch. Gather circle up tightly and finish off securely. Check that you have 6 puffs for body, 10 puffs for each leg and 7 puffs for each arm.
3   Cut elastic in half. Thread each half onto a large-eyed needle and tie a knot 1cm from the end. Thread 10 puffs onto each piece of elastic to form legs, thread both pieces of elastic through the 6 body puffs, then separate elastic and thread 7 puffs on each piece to form arms. Remember to thread contrasting coloured puffs in right places for cuffs or as required. Also, make sure final puffs at ankles and wrists are smooth side out to give a neat finish. Spread puffs evenly along elastic, tie off at wrists and trim ends to 1cm.

Body, arms + legs
cut 36 in main colour
4 in contrast fabric for cuffs
Gathering line

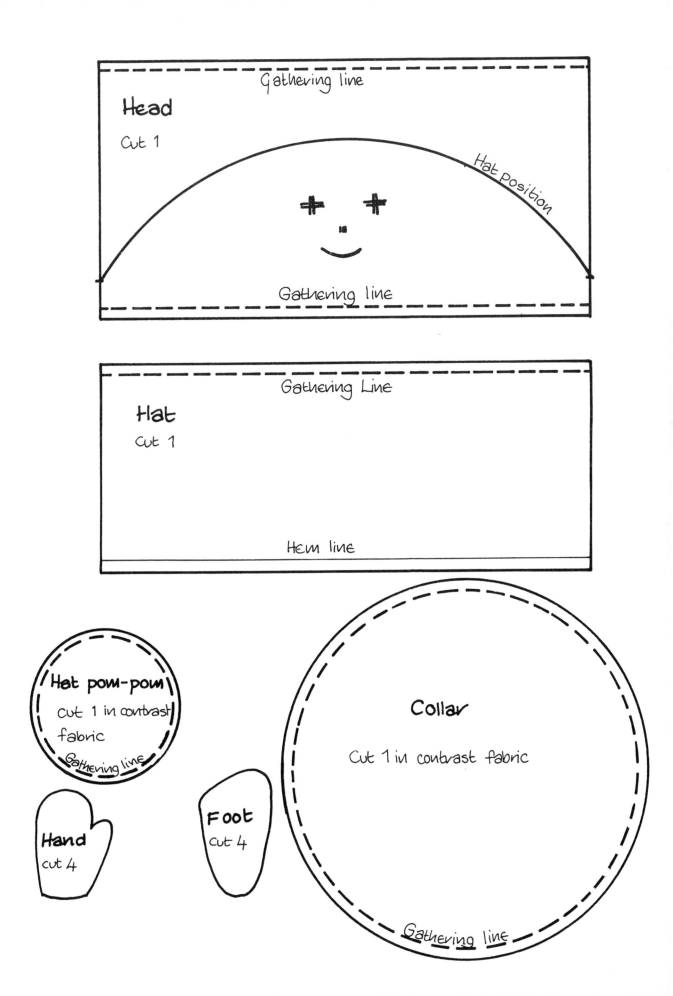

4 Make up large puff from collar pattern and sew securely to top of body, with arms in correct position.

5 Embroider face onto head as indicated, using red for nose and mouth, blue for eyes. Stitch back seam of head. Run gathering threads along top and bottom edges. Pull up one edge, stuff firmly, then pull up other edge tightly and finish off.

6 Join back seam of hat. Gather up top edge tightly. Turn up small hem along bottom edge and stitch with running stitches. Gather pom-pom circle, pull up lightly, stuff firmly, then pull up tightly and fasten off. Attach pom-pom to hat over the gathers. Attach hat to head in position marked on pattern. Sew head securely to collar puff.

7 Oversew 2 hand pieces together neatly, leaving partly open at wrist. Thread end of elastic, with knot, into hand. Sew firmly through felt and knot, closing wrist. Repeat for second hand.

8 Cut small slit in top piece of each foot to insert elastic (near, but not at, heel). Sew each foot together with neat oversewing. Thread elastic through slits and sew securely in place, through knot.

Strawberry Emery
M. Chambers, Bury St Edmunds, Suffolk

An invaluable gift for a lacemaker, this emery serves the practical purpose of keeping brass pins sharp, smooth and tarnish free – and looks pretty at the same time.

Materials
15cm square of red felt
50g emery powder (from suppliers of lace-making materials)
stranded embroidery cotton in yellow and green
scrap of narrow green ribbon
scrap of green felt
matching threads

Method
1 Cut 4 strawberry shapes from red felt using pattern given (Fig 1). Oversew 2 pieces together neatly using matching thread, leaving open between the notches. Turn through, fill firmly with emery powder and sew up opening.

2 Stitch together remaining 2 strawberries, leaving open between Xs. Turn through and stretch slightly. Pull over filled strawberry and sew up opening.

3 Using yellow cotton, work pips on strawberry, starting at the top and working down in a spiral to the point. Work a green stitch at the side of each yellow one.

4 Cut ribbon to required length, fold in half, and stitch to top of strawberry.

5 Cut calyx from green felt using pattern given (Fig 2). Make a small hole in centre to thread ribbon through. Stitch neatly to top of strawberry.

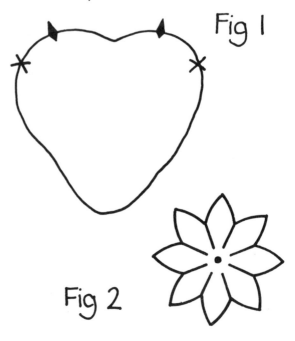

Fig 1

Fig 2

Peg Bag

Mary Belsham, Billingshurst, West Sussex

Another useful but simply made gift – a cheerful peg bag with contrasting lettering applied by using Bondaweb.

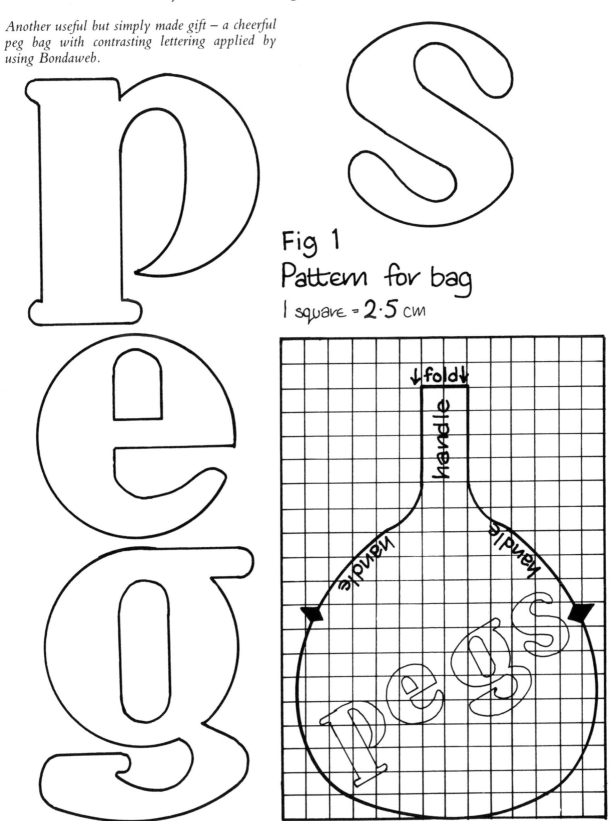

Fig 1
Pattern for bag
1 square = 2·5 cm

Materials

1×0.3m patterned fabric for bag
1×0.3m plain fabric for lining
27×8cm contrasting fabric for letters
27×8cm Bondaweb
tracing paper
carbon paper
2m bias binding (2.5cm wide) to match letters

Method

1   Make paper pattern from diagram (Fig 1), marking notches.
2   Fold each large piece of fabric in half lengthwise. Place pattern on fabric, handle to fold, and cut out once in each fabric. No seam allowances necessary.
3   Press strip of contrasting fabric onto Bondaweb, wrong sides together. Leave to cool. Using pattern given (Fig 2), trace letters, reverse and use carbon paper to transfer in mirror image onto paper side of Bondaweb. Spacing is not important at this stage. Cut out letters neatly and peel off paper.
4   Place letters as desired on front of bag, adhesive side down. Cover with a damp cloth and press with a hot dry iron. Leave to cool. Outline each letter with buttonhole stitch or machine zig-zag. Press.
5   Lay bag and lining wrong sides together. Tack round edges. Bind edges of handle with bias binding between notches. Fold handle in half at centre, right sides out. Tack lower bag edges together below notches, then bind together.

Heart-shaped Brooches

Jennie Ferry, Birkenhead, Merseyside

These tiny heart-shaped brooches (about 4cm across) would be a real hit on St Valentine's Day – or any time of year. The method is easy, but neatness is all-important. Four colour variations are shown in the picture.

Materials

scraps of felt in green, purple and lilac
matching threads
scraps of kapok
small safety pin for each brooch
leather punch (paper punch will do if it is sharp)

Method

1   For green brooch, cut 2 hearts from green felt using pattern given. Start with a knot at A and oversew neatly through B, C, to D, using matching thread (Fig 1).
2   Stuff firmly, then oversew from D to A, finishing with 2 more stitches at A. Do not cut thread.
3   Position safety pin on back as shown (Fig 2). Take needle in at A and bring out at E. Oversew several times at E, sew along pin to F, oversew at F. Take needle in at F, out at E and take a small stitch. Go back to F, take another stitch and cut thread. This ensures pin remains firm when used. NB for left-handed users, pin should face opposite way.
4   Punch 6 small circles of purple felt. Using matching thread, take needle through from back of brooch to position marked 1,

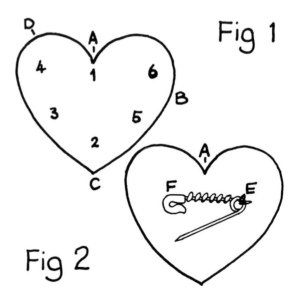

leaving length of thread hanging at back. Make a stitch in centre of purple circle, then take 3 small stitches underneath circle. Cut off thread hanging at back, and stitch other circles in same way, continuing with same thread. Numbers indicate order of stitching. Take thread to back and finish as for green thread.

5 For brooch with half-green and half-purple front, cut 2 green hearts and 1 purple. Cut one green heart and the purple heart in half, down centre. Oversew a green and a purple half together, wrong sides together, using purple thread. This is more accurate than trying to cut round a half heart. Make up as for green brooch, sewing seams with thread to match colour of each half. Attach lilac circles to hide front seam.

Christmas Decorations
Janet Ferry, Birkenhead, Merseyside

Make your own Christmas decorations – these are fun, easy, highly effective and perfect for any Christmas bazaar.

Materials
scraps for felt in red and green
scraps of silver kid
matching thread for felt
'invisible' nylon thread
scraps of kapok
scrap of narrow red ribbon
few sequins
few small beads
silver cord and thread

Method
1 Cut 2 pieces for each heart in required fabric, using patterns given. Oversew seams from A through B and C to D, sewing kid wrong sides together and turning through. Use matching thread for felt, 'invisible' thread for kid.
2 Stuff firmly, oversew D to A, make 3 stitches at A. NB for sizes 3 and 4, add a few small beads to stuffing to weight hearts. To finish off, take thread in at A and out at B, cut off.
3 There are many ways of decorating and hanging the hearts. These are a few suggestions:
Sew on ribbon loop for hanging, and add a small bow on each side.
Sew on sequins using 'invisible' thread. Hang chain of alternate colours in order of size, using 'invisible' thread and 4 small beads between each heart. Hang by a loop of silver cord, tied in a knot at the top.
Wind fine silver thread around a heart, attaching at A and sewing through C to hold in place.

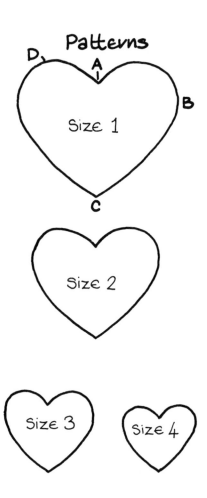

Patterns

Size 1

Size 2

Size 3   Size 4

Play Apron with Book, Crayons and Handkerchief

A. R. Broadburn, Cleethorpes, Humberside

An ideal present for any little girl or boy, the child's apron has specially made pockets for carrying crayons etc. It could easily be adapted to suit a different hobby or game.

Materials

380×330mm main fabric for apron
380×127mm contrasting fabric for pocket
736×50mm contrasting fabric for strings
  and waistband
matching thread
small sketch book
few crayons
handkerchief

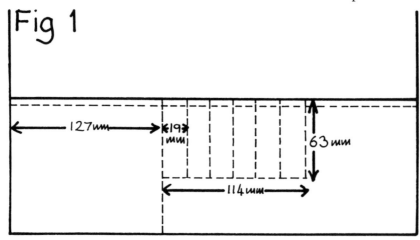

Fig 1

127mm · 19mm · 63mm · 114mm

stitching. Neaten apron sides the same way.
2 To make small pockets in the large pocket, topstitch through both layers, following the measurements in Fig 1.
3 Gather top of apron with running stitches until it measures 280mm.
4 To make strings and waistband, fold fabric strip in half lengthways and press under raw edges. Place gathered top of apron inside waistband, matching centres (Fig 2). Tack. Topstitch whole length of strings and waistband (including ends of strings). Place book, crayons and handkerchief in pockets.

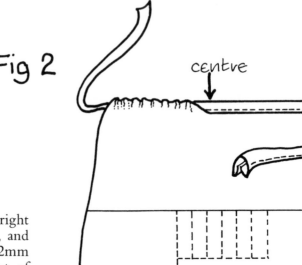

Fig 2

centre

How to join waistband to apron

Method

1 Place pocket on bottom of apron, right side of pocket to wrong side of apron, and machine along bottom edge with 12mm seam allowance. Turn pocket to front of apron and press. Neaten top of pocket by turning under 3mm, then 6mm, then top-

Knitting Bag and Needle Roll

Karen Rowe, Ware, Hertfordshire

A practical present to keep knitting clean and tidy, and knitting needles securely out of harm's way. Both are made simply and well, to withstand plenty of wear.

Materials

For the needle roll
60×83cm cotton fabric
matching thread
50cm narrow cord or ribbon
For the bag
76×46cm cotton fabric
28cm diameter circle cotton fabric
matching thread
2m narrow cord
4 eyelets (optional)
25cm diameter circle card (optional)

Method

TO MAKE NEEDLE ROLL

1 Turn narrow double hems along short sides of fabric and machine stitch. With right sides together, fold over 28cm (see Fig 1) and machine side seams with 1cm allowance. Press seams open and turn through to right side.
2 Turn remaining raw edges into narrow double hem and tack. Topstitch round 3 sides as shown in Fig 2, including over tacking.
3 Machine rows of stitching 2–3cm apart to form channels for knitting needles as shown. Vary the sizes of channels to accommodate different sizes of needle.
4 Stitch centre of cord or ribbon in position indicated at one side of needle holder. Fill roll with knitting needles, fold top down over them, roll case up and fasten with cord.

TO MAKE BAG

1 With right sides together, match short sides of rectangle and machine stitch with 1cm seam allowance. Neaten seam and press to one side. Open and make into 'tube'.
2 Fix 2 eyelets 2cm from top edge (see Fig 3) and 1cm each side of seam, following instructions on packet. Or make 2 small buttonholes. Fix 2 more eyelets (or button-

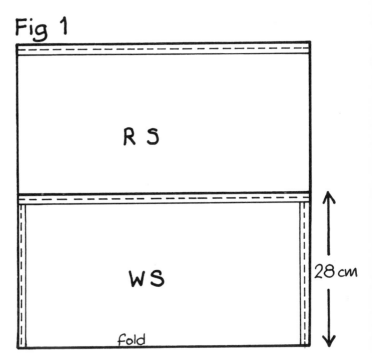

Fig 1

RS

WS

fold

28 cm

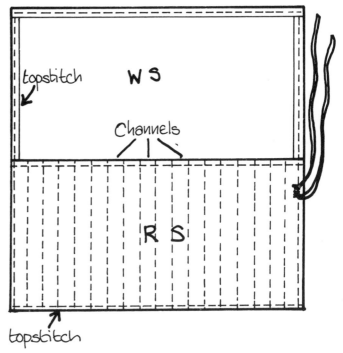

Fig 2

topstitch

WS

Channels

RS

topstitch

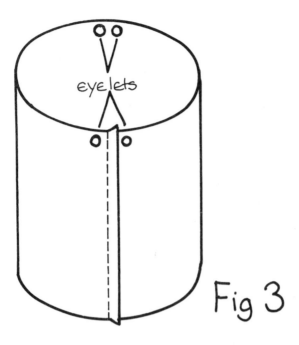

Fig 3

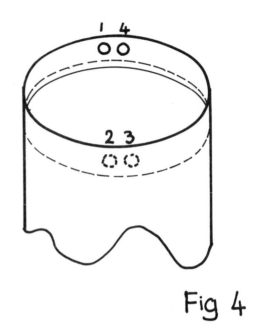

Fig 4

holes) opposite first ones, also on top edge.
3 Turn top edge over 5mm to inside and press. Fold down a further 3cm, bringing eyelets to inside and forming a casing round top of bag for cord. Machine round casing.
4 Thread one end of cord into eyelet 1 (see Fig 4), through casing past eyelets 2, 3, 4 and 1, coming out at 2 (the second time round). Thread back in at 3, continue to 4, bring cord out and fasten ends together.
5 Fit circle of fabric into bottom of bag, right sides together, and stitch round seam with 1cm allowance. Press and trim seam to 5mm. Turn bag through to right side. With wrong sides together, stitch 5mm in from circular seam to reinforce base (and make it neater and flatter). If required, a circle of card may be inserted into base of bag.

Hand-printed Scarf

J. M. Wynn-Jones, Eastbourne, East Sussex

This pretty scarf is made from pink polyester and printed with the leaves of bindweed, but any soft draping fabric and other leaves could be used to similar effect.

Materials

one piece of soft draping fabric – at least 66cm square for a square scarf or 20.3×127cm for a long scarf
a selection of Dylon Colour Fun Fabric Paint – with a mix of red, yellow, black and white most colours are available
leaves or feathers

Method

1 Cut the fabric to size and place it right side up on some clean newspaper.
2 Place leaf or feather face down on another piece of newspaper (this should be larger than the leaf) and carefully paint the leaf back with the fabric paint.
3 Lift the leaf and place it ink side down on the fabric. Put a clean piece of newspaper on top and press it down firmly.
4 Peel off the newspaper and then the leaf or feather, revealing the print.
5 Repeat steps 2–4 until you have a pleasing pattern and then leave the scarf to dry.
6 To fix cover with a clean cloth and press firmly with a hot iron for 2 or 3 minutes.
7 To finish the scarf turn under and slip-stitch a narrow hem. Press the hem flat.

144